CROWN AND PARLIAMENT

DANCING ROUND THE MAYPOLE
ON MAY DAY MORNING

Crown and Parliament

1485-1688

R. J. UNSTEAD

with drawings by Stanley Herbert

LONDON
A & C BLACK LTD

A HISTORY OF BRITAIN

1 THE MEDIEVAL SCENE, 787–1485
2 CROWN AND PARLIAMENT, 1485–1688
3 THE RISE OF GREAT BRITAIN, 1688–1837
4 A CENTURY OF CHANGE, 1837–TODAY

Also by R. J. Unstead

LOOKING AT HISTORY
PEOPLE IN HISTORY
MEN AND WOMEN IN HISTORY
LOOKING AT ANCIENT HISTORY
EARLY TIMES
THE STORY OF BRITAIN
TRAVEL BY ROAD
HOUSES
MONASTERIES
CASTLES
LIVING IN A CASTLE
LIVING IN A CRUSADER LAND
LIVING IN A MEDIEVAL CITY
LIVING IN A MEDIEVAL VILLAGE
LIVING IN AZTEC TIMES
LIVING IN SAMUEL PEPYS' LONDON
LIVING IN THE ELIZABETHAN COURT
LIVING IN POMPEII
LIVING IN ANCIENT EGYPT
EGYPT AND MESOPOTAMIA
GREECE AND ROME

THIS IMPRESSION 1979

ISBN 0 7136 1842 6

PRINTED PHOTOLITHO IN GREAT BRITAIN BY
J. W. ARROWSMITH LTD., BRISTOL

FOREWORD

In the five books of this series I have tried to describe simply the chief events and personalities in Britain's history so that they will interest the reader and help him to understand how and why certain happenings have taken place. Also, at a time when it is fashionable in some quarters to belittle Britain's achievements in the past and to doubt her place in the future, I have tried to show that whereas Britain has often acted foolishly or badly, her history shows the persistence of ideals which good men have lived by since Alfred's day.

In this story of a thousand years it is the character of a people that comes through; I hope that the reader will recognise this character and be glad.

R. J. Unstead

CONTENTS

Part One : The Tudors

1. The Recovery of England 9
2. "The Great Harry" 12
3. The Quarrel with the Pope 17
4. The Reformation in England 27
5. The World Enlarged 39
6. The Reign of Elizabeth 50
7. Elizabeth's England 73
8. The Elizabethans at Home 80
9. At Work and Play 90

Part Two : The Stuarts

10. King James I 106
11. Dispute between King and Parliament 114
12. The Civil War 131

13. Parliament versus Army 150

14. (i) The Commonwealth 156

(ii) The Lord Protector 161

15. King Charles II 167

16. The Last Stuart King 177

17. Englishmen Abroad 182

18. Two Portraits

(i) A Love Story 187

(ii) The Prudent Cavalier 194

Summary 202

Index 205

ACKNOWLEDGEMENTS

Most of the drawings reproduced in this book are by Stanley Herbert. Acknowledgement is made for the use of drawings on pages 11 (a and b), 88, 96 (a), 128 and 163 (a and b) from *English Costume in the Age of Elizabeth* by Iris Brooke; on page 128 (a) and 129 (b) from *English Costume in the Seventeenth Century* by Iris Brooke; on pages 22, 75, 96 (b), 159, 160, 188 and 189 from *Makers of History* by Emmeline Garnett; on pages 82 (a, b and c) and 197 (a and b) from *English Furniture* by John Gloag; on pages 44 and 186 from *Travel by Sea* by R. J. Hoare; on page 68 (a and b) from *London* by John Hayes; on page 199 (b) from *Isaac Newton* by Patrick Moore; on pages 74 (a and b), 76, 77 (b), 138, 139, 142, 180 and 193 from *Looking at History* by R. J. Unstead; on page 158 (a) from *People in History* by R. J. Unstead; on page 190 from *Travel by Road* by R. J. Unstead; on page 130 from *A Second Book of Architecture* by G. H. Reed; and on pages 127 (b), 155 and 156 from *Black's Children's Encyclopaedia*; the drawings on pages 31 (b), 58 (b), 73 (b), 92 (a), 145, 149, 150, 151, 158 (b) are by S. A. Edwards and on pages 99, and 100(b) by Edward Mortelmans.

Holbein's Portrait of a Merchant, which appears on the cover of this book, is reproduced from the collotype print published by the Pallas Gallery, London.

PART ONE

THE TUDORS

CHAPTER I

THE RECOVERY OF ENGLAND

1485–1509

THE TUDOR ROSE

WHEN the victory at Bosworth Field brought the crown of England to Henry Tudor, none of those who cheered the new king could have been certain that the Wars of the Roses were over and that a new age had begun. To prudent men, it must have seemed that Bosworth was only one more battle in the wearisome struggle between York and Lancaster; but, in fact, the wary-eyed victor was to keep his kingdom for twenty-four years and to leave it wealthier and more secure than it had been for centuries.

After the Wars of the Roses

At first, Henry's position was far from promising. The Tudor claim to the throne was so thin that, without going into details, he merely declared himself the rightful king of England and married Elizabeth of York, Edward IV's daughter, to settle the feud. However, there were still Yorkists prepared to rebel rather than accept a Lancastrian on the throne, especially as their lands and former winnings were forfeit. They might be weak for the moment, but help could come from France, from the Duchess of Burgundy who ruled Flanders, from James IV of Scotland or from the lawless barons of Ireland.

Faced with this situation, Henry went steadily to work, as though he had long thought out the steps he must take to keep the throne. He had not the brilliant gifts nor the showmanship to become a popular figure, but he knew, as his people knew, that there could be no good government unless the king was strong. To be strong, a king must have money.

HENRY VII

WEALTHY WRONG-DOERS WERE SUMMONED BEFORE THE COURT OF STAR CHAMBER

Keeping the nobles in order

First, however, the country needed to regain respect for the laws of the land, and this could not happen while lords kept private armies to support themselves and their friends. The nobles were made to swear an oath that they would not cause riots, hold unlawful meetings or keep retainers arrayed in " livery "—the name given to private badges and uniforms. " Maintenance ", the custom whereby lords supported their servants in the law-courts, was forbidden, and the bribing of judges and juries was checked. Wealthy wrong-doers were summoned before the King's Council, meeting in the Star Chamber, where punishment almost always took the form of crippling fines.

Henry's lawyers squeezed the last penny out of those who were fined ; rich men were encouraged to make gifts and " benevolences " to the royal purse, as well as " loans " which were never repaid. Costly foreign wars were avoided, and Henry only invaded France in order to extract a vast sum from the French king who was willing to buy him off. With money in the Treasury, Henry could keep the nobles in check, since they knew he could hire a powerful army

PERKIN WARBECK

to support his rule. As time went by, Henry's mania for wealth caused his officers to be hated by the well-to-do classes.

Henry VII's skill in government

But if he grasped wealth, Henry also created it. Half a century of bad government at home and disputes abroad had brought business into a shaky condition. Foreign merchants controlled much of the trade, the powerful Hanse League of North Germany kept English merchants out of the Baltic, and the Mediterranean was closed to all but the Genoese and Venetians. Most of the cargoes in and out of English ports were carried in foreign ships, even wool to Flanders and Italy, and wine from Bordeaux.

By patience and crafty skill, Henry gradually overcame these difficulties. He encouraged the merchants, especially of London and Bristol, revived shipbuilding and restored the carrying-trade to English vessels. The Hanse merchants were made to yield ground, and even Venice and Florence had to admit English shipping to the Mediterranean.

Abroad, Henry outwitted his enemies, even when they supported Perkin Warbeck, a youth who pretended to be the younger of the Princes murdered in the Tower. An alliance was formed with Spain, through the marriage of Henry's son, Arthur, to Catherine of Aragon ; treaties were made with France and Burgundy, while Scotland was won over by the marriage between the king's daughter, Margaret Tudor, and James IV.

Thus, when Henry VII died in 1509, England was a different kingdom from the weary, sullen land of 1485. The King was able to leave to his second son all that he himself had lacked—enormous wealth, a secure throne, obedient nobles in a lively, vigorous kingdom, and the prospect of a glittering future. What he could not leave was his own cautious common-sense.

A MERCHANT AND HIS WIFE

CHAPTER 2

"THE GREAT HARRY"

The young king, Henry VIII

At eighteen years of age, Henry VIII was the handsomest monarch in Europe. Moreover, his talents were as brilliant as his appearance, for in wrestling, jousting, horsemanship, archery and tennis, there were few to equal him. He was also a fine musician, a composer, poet, writer and an expert in the religious discussions that occupied men of his day. His jovial manner and royal bearing delighted the people, and he at once increased his popularity by executing two of his father's most detested ministers. Then he married Catherine of Aragon, twenty-four-year-old widow of his brother Arthur. The lavish display of wealth at the coronation and at the royal wedding seemed to be a foretaste of glories to come.

WAR WITH FRANCE

All eyes were turned on young King Harry, Henry VIII, and it was not surprising that he should want to cut a more dashing figure than his father. He had money and high spirits, and his people were in the mood for the glory and loot of a foreign adventure. Where else should they turn but to the ancient enemy across the Channel? Henry renewed the claim of English kings to the French throne, at a time when France, deadly rival of Spain, was trying to seize the state of Milan, in northern Italy.

AN ARMOURED KNIGHT OF THE SIXTEENTH CENTURY

HENRY VIII ENCOURAGED THE SHIPBUILDERS

Vain and ambitious though he was, Henry had enough sense not to plunge into war without following his father's example of keeping the Channel safe. He encouraged the shipbuilders, and took a close interest in their craft.

Early in his reign, a fine ship of 1,500 tons was added to the Navy and its name, " The Great Harry ", exactly described the people's regard for their king. In an age when men were violent, greedy and heartless, they wanted a king who looked the part, who spent freely, and ruled them like some rough sea-captain striding his deck, masterful and brutal.

In pursuit of glory, Henry crossed to France (1513) with an expensive army, and fought a battle at which the French knights galloped away so fast that it was known as the *Battle of Spurs*. This was no Agincourt, and, ironically enough, a far greater victory was won at home. The Scots, untroubled by the fact that their queen was Henry's sister, invaded the northern counties. Queen Catherine collected an army under the Earl of Surrey, who outmanoeuvred the Scots and won a crushing victory—the last for the longbow and one of the first with cannon—at *Flodden*, where King James IV and many of his nobles were killed.

Scots defeated at Flodden

Thus, the year closed in triumph. Europe had been informed that England was once more a country to reckon with, under a dashing king and an upstart Chancellor.

CARDINAL WOLSEY

The new Chancellor, Thomas Wolsey, was the brilliant son of an Ipswich merchant who sent him to Oxford and into the Church, the route to fortune for able young men without noble parents. His energy and ability brought him to Court as a royal chaplain, where the king noticed his talent and raised him to the Council.

The French war gave Wolsey his chance, for the King wanted a first-class man of affairs to manage the kingdom, leaving himself free to play the gay and popular monarch. While Henry passed his nights at banquets and revels and his days at the hunt, the tournament and a hundred other things that pleased him, Wolsey attended to more important business. He served the king and at the same time enriched himself, chiefly by obtaining high positions in the Church. Lord Chancellor, Archbishop of York, Bishop of Winchester, Abbot of St. Albans, Cardinal and Papal Legate (Ambassador), Wolsey even began to entertain hopes of becoming Pope. With his vast income, three palaces and 700 servants, he lived in a style that outshone the King himself.

PIKES WERE USED BY FOOT-SOLDIERS

HENRY MEETS FRANCIS I AT THE "FIELD OF THE CLOTH OF GOLD"

WOLSEY THE DIPLOMAT

Peace with France

Peace was made with France, and the king's younger sister Mary, a girl of seventeen, was married to the French king, a widower of fifty-two, who inconveniently died the next year. However, Wolsey was determined to advance his master's, and his own, importance by dangling England's support between the rivals—Francis I, the new king of France, and Charles V of Spain, who became Holy Roman Emperor.

War was certain to break out between these two, and Wolsey arranged a meeting between Francis and Henry near Calais, where both youthful kings showed off their wealth so monstrously that the occasion was known as the *Field of the Cloth of Gold* (1520). However, this was no more than a showpiece in the diplomatic game. It was certain that England would side with Charles V, Catherine's nephew, ruler of Flanders and therefore of the wool trade. As

A SHILLING OF THE REIGN OF HENRY VIII

Holy Roman Emperor, Charles could get Wolsey elected Pope.

A second war with France (1522-23) amounted to no more than costly marching to and fro with the usual slaughter and looting. Meanwhile, in Italy, Charles V won so complete a victory over the French at *Pavia*, where King Francis was captured, that England's support was no longer needed. On two occasions, Charles did nothing to help Wolsey become Pope.

This set-back revealed chinks in the armour of the great man but, as long as Wolsey held the royal favour, no one could touch him. Henry now set him an impossible task—no less than the annulment of the marriage to Queen Catherine, aunt of the most powerful king in Christendom, who had the Pope in his power.

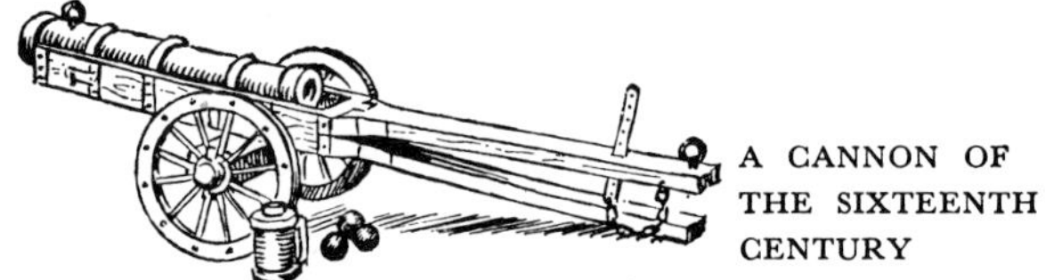

A CANNON OF THE SIXTEENTH CENTURY

CHAPTER 3

THE QUARREL WITH THE POPE

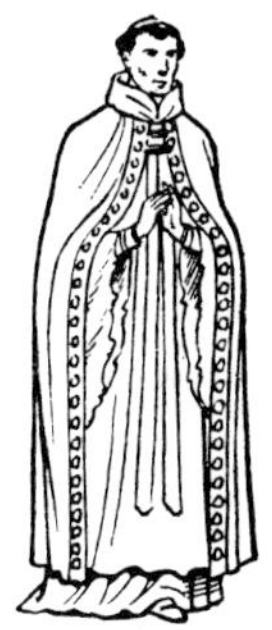
A PRIEST

THE CHURCH

We must pause here to look at the position of the Church.

As in medieval times, the Church was powerful and rich. Besides the parish priests, the wandering friars, the chantry priests who prayed for the dead, the 7000 monks and nuns who had withdrawn from the world, there was a host of clerks in " minor orders ", some of them rogues and even criminals. Above these was a class of higher clergy, from canons and deans to abbots and bishops, many of whom drew incomes for duties they never performed in places which they never visited.

On every side, men toiled on broad Church lands to produce wealth for men like Wolsey, who drew £10,000 a year from his various appointments.

A MONK

Thus, although there were good and sincere men among the clergy, it was generally felt that the Church had become too rich and worldly. The monasteries, in particular, were a target for public dislike, for they seemed to provide a fat living for monks who gave little in return. The friars, once loved by the poor, were now looked on as no better than rascally pedlars.

The authority of the Pope was supreme in every country of Western Europe. Anyone who dared to question his rule or to disagree with the official views of the Catholic Church was declared a *heretic*, to be punished by death unless he humbled himself and took back all that he had said. From all countries,

A FRIAR

JOHN CALVIN

including England, large sums of money were regularly sent to Rome in the form of Papal taxes and collections.

MARTIN LUTHER

The Church had always required people to do penance for their sins, and the custom had grown up of allowing them to avoid punishment by paying money for a written pardon called an *Indulgence.* About 1515, the cost of building the great church of St. Peter in Rome was so heavy that a special sale of Indulgences was arranged, and the friar Tetzel was sent to Germany to organise the sales. He came to Wittenberg, where a university professor, a friar named Martin Luther, had already decided that these sales were frauds. Luther opposed Tetzel and having written 95 arguments against Indulgences, he nailed his paper to a church door. (Tetzel's form of preaching was later condemned by the Roman Catholic Church.)

This daring act caused great excitement in Germany, where there was a strong feeling for reform. Luther's paper was printed and handed from place to place ; furious arguments broke out and many people supported the bold friar. Luther was led on to attack the Church and even the Pope himself, until he was declared a heretic and excommunicated. By this time, he had become a popular hero and he hurled the Bull (or paper) of Excommunication into a bonfire at Wittenberg.

THE CHURCH OF ST. PETER, AT ROME

Other preachers followed Luther's example, or went even further in their protests against the old customs and beliefs. *John Calvin*, a Frenchman, would have no clergy at all, only ministers chosen by their congregations. This type of church, called Presbyterian, was established first in Geneva. " Calvinism ", a hard, strict religion, attracted many followers, and later found favour in Scotland.

John Calvin, 1509–64

Those who opposed or protested against the Catholic beliefs came to be called *Protestants* and their ideas became so widespread that the whole movement was known as the *Reformation* because it had sprung from a desire to *reform* the older religion.

Protestantism made very little headway in Spain and in Italy but, north of the Alps, in Germany, Switzerland, Flanders and, later on, in England and Scotland, a majority adopted the new religion, while some brave spirits clung to the old faith, often in secret and always in peril.

Despite widespread contempt for the clergy and envy of the Church's wealth, England took little interest in Luther and his teachings. Indeed, Henry, who regarded himself as a faithful son of the Church, actually wrote an answer to Luther's 95 arguments, for which the Pope rewarded him with the title " Fidei Defensor "—Defender of the Faith.

When Henry married his brother's widow, Catherine was 24, not beautiful but attractive, lively and popular. She spoke English well, was musical, a good dancer, and, above all, a devoted wife and Catholic.

LUTHER BURNED THE PAPER WHICH EXCOMMUNICATED HIM FROM THE CHURCH

POPE CLEMENT VII

With all his faults, Henry seems to have loved and respected Catherine for many years, though all their sons and daughters died in babyhood, except Mary. Now, in 1527, the Queen had been married for 18 years and, at the age of 42, was considered elderly and unlikely to have any more children. The king was 36, beginning to grow stout, but still full of vigour, and much more serious about his kingly duties. More than anything in the world, he wanted a son to follow him, for no queen had ever ruled England.

Even so, there were no important Yorkists left, and the country was staunch for the Tudors. Henry might have resigned himself to his faithful wife, had he not fallen in love with one of the Queen's ladies-in-waiting. Anne Boleyn, dark-eyed with shining black hair, was the daughter of Lord Rochford and niece of the Duke of Norfolk, though the old nobility regarded her family as jumped-up newcomers.

Insolent to those whom she despised, Anne so fascinated Henry with her pert gaiety that, finding she was not to be won without marriage, he determined to get rid of Catherine.

Although the Church did not allow divorce, Popes had, from time to time, obligingly declared that a marriage did not exist. It was Wolsey's task to persuade the Pope that this marriage must be annulled, i.e. cancelled, on the grounds that it should never have taken place. The more Henry thought about it, the more he convinced himself that Heaven had never approved his marriage to a brother's widow.

HENRY VIII

ANNE BOLEYN SO FASCINATED HENRY THAT HE DETERMINED TO GET RID OF CATHERINE

Unfortunately, Pope Clement VII now found himself in a difficult position. He had enough trouble on hand with Luther and the German princes not to wish to offend the English king, yet he was virtually a prisoner of Charles V, nephew of Queen Catherine. So the Pope played for time and gave no answer.

As delay followed delay, King Henry turned furiously on Wolsey for his failure to achieve the impossible. The great Cardinal was speedily ruined and died on his way to London to face trial for high treason.

THE BREAK WITH ROME

More heartless and self-willed with every set-back to his hopes, Henry bent all his energies to have his way. The Pope had refused him; then the Pope, and all that was the Pope's, must learn the power of an absolute king in his secure island. The clergy were brought to heel and fined a huge sum for obeying Wolsey ; many of their money-making " abuses " were stopped and payments to Rome were suspended.

Persecution of Protestants by More

All this time, however, there was no sympathy for Protestant reformers, and the new Chancellor, Sir Thomas More, showed more vigour than Wolsey in searching out heretics and burning them at Smithfield.

After three more years, the King's patience was exhausted. Parliament, solidly on his side, passed a law abolishing appeals to Rome on the subject of marriage. The new Archbishop of Canterbury, *Thomas Cranmer*, declared that the marriage to Catherine was illegal, and Henry announced that he had already married Anne in secret.

Anne's charm existed for no one but the King. The Court detested her insolent manner and the Catholic nobles suspected her circle of holding Lutheran opinions. The Londoners saw in her a cheap little schemer who had ousted their Queen, and they failed to raise a cheer as she went by to her magnificent coronation. A woman in the crowd called out an evil name, and some muttered that she had put a spell on the king by witchcraft.

It was soon known that Anne would shortly bear a child, perhaps the longed-for son. Any children that Anne might bear were declared legal heirs to the throne. Next, the Act of Supremacy stated that the King, not the Pope, was " the Supreme Head on earth, under God, of the Church of England ".

This tremendous decision to separate England from the Roman Church to which she had belonged for a thousand years, could not have been made without the support of a Parliament and people holding little respect for the Pope who, they said, " hath no more power in England than any other foreign bishop ".

MANY " HERETICS " WERE BURNED AT SMITHFIELD

SIR THOMAS MORE WENT TO THE SCAFFOLD RATHER THAN ADMIT THAT A LAYMAN MIGHT BE HEAD OF THE CHURCH

Only a few sincere Catholics died rather than agree that a layman might be Head of the Church. Sir Thomas More, a scholar known throughout Europe and one of the noblest men of his age, went to the scaffold. Ten Charterhouse monks were hanged, and Bishop John Fisher was beheaded. All the rest of the clergy—bishops and parish priests alike—accepted the oath.

THE MONASTERIES

Thomas Cromwell, the "Vicar-General"

The King's right-hand man was now *Thomas Cromwell*, the dreaded "Vicar-General". Like Wolsey, Cromwell was not nobly born, but had risen through ability and guile from merchant, shady lawyer and money-lender, to secretary to Wolsey. Now he stepped into the King's favour by promising to make him "the richest prince in Christendom". He would deal with the monasteries.

Generally speaking, people felt that the religious houses had outlived their usefulness. Many were poor and badly run, with fewer than a dozen monks or nuns; others were so occupied with the financial muddle of their property that there was insufficient

TWO NUNS

attention to religious life. Everywhere the numbers of monks and nuns were declining.

Cromwell's agents went round to the smaller monasteries to make enquiries, and their reports, known as the Black Book of the Monasteries, naturally stressed every instance of broken rules. Despite dark hints of scandalous behaviour by the monks, it seemed in truth that many had become careless and greedy rather than wicked.

In 1536, however, when it received the damning report of Cromwell's agents, Parliament passed a law closing all religious houses with incomes of less than £200 a year, and giving their property to the King.

THE PILGRIMAGE OF GRACE

Smaller religious houses are closed

There were 376 of these smaller monasteries and all, except about 100, were closed. The monks and nuns, numbering some 2,000 (an average of less than 8 to each religious house), were given pensions or were sent to larger houses.

A quarter of the monasteries closed were in Lincolnshire and Yorkshire, counties far from London, where ways had not changed so rapidly as in the south, and where monasteries were still popular. The loss of their local abbeys shocked both the gentry and common folk. Most of them still held to the old

CROMWELL'S AGENTS INSPECTED THE SMALLER MONASTERIES

ONE SERIOUS REVOLT, IN YORKSHIRE, WAS CALLED THE PILGRIMAGE OF GRACE

religion, and they also had various grievances about Enclosures and the behaviour of Cromwell's officers. A feeble rising in Lincolnshire was followed by a serious revolt in Yorkshire, which spread further afield. Led by Robert Aske and others of good family, a force of 30,000 men captured York and gathered at Doncaster, demanding the removal of Cromwell, the abolition of heresy (i.e. Protestantism) and the restoration of the monasteries. They declared that this was no rebellion, but a pilgrimage—the *Pilgrimage of Grace* under the banner of Christ.

Revolt in Yorkshire

The last thing that Henry wanted was civil war, and, for the moment, he had no force large enough to crush the rising, but he judged the situation perfectly. He knew that the rebels had no popular leader and did not want war, so he showed mildness and goodwill, offering pardon if they dispersed to their homes. Then he pounced. The leaders, including Aske, four abbots, and about 200 others were arrested and executed.

THE END OF THE MONASTERIES

Once again, the King had shown who was master of England. One by one, the great abbots began to surrender their abbeys, tempted perhaps by the thought that, if they were doomed, they would do better to secure pensions than be turned out penniless.

Larger monasteries are closed

Between 1536 and 1540, all the monasteries were closed, and their lands, buildings, silver plate and jewelled vessels became the property of the king. In return, an abbot received a pension of about £250 a year, which was a large income. Priors had £16, and monks amounts varying from £13 to just over £6—enough to support life comfortably, and it seems that the pensions were, in fact, paid as regularly as could be expected. Very few abbots resisted the seizure, and those who did so were arrested for treason and executed, sometimes with disgusting barbarity. The mild old Abbot of Glastonbury was dragged through the town on a hurdle, hanged, and his severed head was stuck up over the gate of the abbey.

The king needed money badly, so the monastic gold and silver went into the Treasury, the valuable lead roofs were broken down and sold, and the lands and properties went to the highest, or luckiest, bidders, since the king gave little away. With the market suddenly flooded, prices were cheap and a large class of people—landowners, successful merchants and many a rich burgess, secured bargains at knock-down prices. They and their families, therefore, would never support religious changes which might lead to a handing-back of the monastic lands. Henry thus had an influential class entirely on his side.

THE RUINS OF FOUNTAINS ABBEY TODAY

CHAPTER 4

THE REFORMATION IN ENGLAND

BIBLES WERE SO VALUABLE THAT THEY WERE CHAINED

To understand the religious struggles of this period, we must be clear about the main differences between Catholics and Protestants. The Catholics (and some Protestants) believed in *The Apostolic Succession*, i.e. that priests had special powers passed to them through the ages from the Apostles, and these powers, allowed them to bring salvation to ordinary people. Protestants would not accept the authority of the Pope. They said that complicated ceremonies and services in Latin were wrong, because people should read the Bible for themselves and take part in services. Some, but not all, Protestants felt that clergymen were unnecessary and that church music, stained glass, images, pictures and statues were wicked inventions of the Devil. Great argument took place upon the doctrines, or teachings, of religion, as to whether priests should marry, whether Confession was necessary, and particularly over *Transubstantiation*, the belief that, at Holy Communion, the bread and wine are changed into the body and blood of Christ.

Catholics held firm to the old beliefs and the absolute rule of the Pope, whereas there were—and still are—many shades of Protestant opinion. At this time, both sides agreed on one thing, that there must be no tolerance or freedom for the other side.

THE INVENTION OF PRINTING MADE IT POSSIBLE TO PRODUCE BOOKS MORE EASILY

THE BIBLE IN ENGLISH

Meanwhile, the majority of English people had no sympathy with Protestant reformers. They were quite content with their old religion, now that they had ousted the Pope and closed the monasteries. The King himself was turning back to Catholic beliefs, though he allowed Cromwell to have English Bibles placed in churches.

Tyndale's translation of the New Testament

Earlier in the reign, *William Tyndale* had gone abroad to translate and publish the New Testament, which was smuggled into England, where, for a time, copies were seized and burned, just as Tyndale himself was burned when he fell into the grip of the Inquisition in Flanders. In 1534, *Miles Coverdale*, an ex-friar, used Tyndale's work to complete the translation of the whole Bible. Archbishop Cranmer had this version revised by *John Rogers*, alias Mathew, so that, from 1539, it was " Mathew's Bible " that was read in church.

THE END OF CROMWELL

The marriage with Anne Boleyn, for which the king had risked so much, went wrong in less time than it had taken to arrange. Instead of a son, Anne's child was a redhaired girl, christened Elizabeth, and, later, two boys were born dead. Had they lived, their mother would have lived too, but perhaps she rejoiced too loudly when poor Queen Catherine died in 1536, or perhaps Henry's conscience was stirred by Anne's cruel laughter ; more likely, he was already tired of her and willing to listen to those who hated her. At all events, Anne Boleyn was suddenly arrested and charged with having made love to various gentlemen of the Court. Although it is difficult to believe that she could have been so foolish, she was tried and beheaded.

WILLIAM TYNDALE

Henry celebrated the occasion with a banquet, and, before a month was out, married *Jane Seymour*, a maid-of-honour to the late Queen. Within a year, she, too, was dead, a few days after the birth of her son, Edward.

JANE SEYMOUR

In 1539, in face of danger from France and Spain, Cromwell was urging Henry to make an alliance with the Protestant rulers of Germany, by marrying *Anne of Cleves*, a German princess. When all was arranged, the lady arrived in England and proved to be, not the beauty whom Cromwell had described, but an exceedingly plain and rather dull person. With a bad grace, Henry went through with the marriage, but Cromwell was ruined, all the more so because it was clear that France and Spain were not going to join forces.

As usual, Henry bided his time and then struck savagely. Cromwell was arrested, charged with

ANNE BOLEYN WAS ARRESTED, TRIED AND EXECUTED

treason and executed. The marriage with Anne of Cleves was "cancelled", and she retired with a pension, on which she lived cheerfully for the rest of her life. Once more, Henry was looking for a wife, and he found her in *Catherine Howard*, a beautiful girl, related to the Catholic Duke of Norfolk.

Henry marries Catherine Howard, a Catholic

This triumph for the Catholics was short-lived, for it was soon proved that Catherine Howard was no innocent maiden, and, since her offences were called treason, her lovely head was severed from her body.

The mere mention of treason was enough to condemn man or woman, and Henry struck left and right at any who roused his suspicions, for his temper, never certain, was now inflamed by ill-health and the pain from a vast ulcer in his swollen leg. His sixth wife, *Catherine Parr*, was a discreet widow who managed to outlive the old tyrant.

THE THIRD WAR WITH FRANCE, 1544–45

The Pope had not ceased trying to bring the disobedient island back to his rule and, from 1542, it seemed likely that France would carry out his wishes by invading England. In the north, an attack would also be launched from Scotland, where James V had married a French princess.

Henry bestirred himself with some of his old energy. A small English force routed the Scots at *Solway Moss*, and, within a month, James V died of shame. His French wife became Regent, for their daughter, Mary Queen of Scots, was a baby, only a few days old. Next, Henry heaved his huge bulk into armour, crossed the Channel at the head of an army he could ill afford, and captured Boulogne.

This success only increased the danger, since the French fleet was preparing for invasion. Moreover,

A LADY OF THE SIXTEENTH CENTURY

the enthusiasm with which English seamen boarded neutral ships and seized goods in the Channel, so offended the Emperor that he ended the shaky alliance with Henry, and seemed likely to join France.

CATHERINE PARR

At this stage, England was seen to be united behind the King. Every seaman was called up for service, every able-bodied man was ready at an hour's notice to serve in the militia, beacons were prepared to signal the alarm and, all along the coasts, forts were manned and stocked with cannons. The people were ready to fight and to pay the cost of defence.

When the French fleet, reinforced with Mediterranean war-galleys, drew near the coast, it was roughly treated by the English navy, headed by the "Great Harry". The few landing-parties that got ashore were beaten off before serious danger could develop and, by the end of 1545, the French had had enough.

THE REFORMATION IN EDWARD VI'S REIGN

1547–1553

So far, Protestant ideas had entered England through exiles from abroad and through the accident of the King's quarrel with Rome. Luther's views had little appeal to most Englishmen and none at all to Henry, but the marriage problem had led, step by step, to changes which encouraged the handful of reformers. The Pope's authority had gone, and the monasteries, too. The King, though still obstinately Catholic, was Head of the Church in which an English Bible was read and some English prayers said.

Though Henry was quite ready to execute some for being too Protestant and others for being too Catholic, there were supporters of both religions at

BEACONS ON HILL TOPS WERE USED TO SEND MESSAGES OVER GREAT DISTANCES

Court who managed to keep their heads on their shoulders. They were already preparing for the day when the King must die. He was still only in his fifties, but was already old ; his brain was undimmed, but his great body had become a bloated, diseased mass of pain. Dying, Henry made it clear that the country was to be ruled by a carefully chosen council of both Catholics and reformers, until his little son was sixteen years old.

Death of Henry VIII

PROTECTOR SOMERSET

Hardly was Henry dead, than Edward VI's uncle became Duke of Somerset and Protector of the realm. Somerset was an interesting character. As greedy for wealth and Church property as any of the class which had risen rapidly through royal favour, he was a sincere Protestant who wanted to be fair to the poor and more reasonable than most in matters of religion.

Somerset and his friends, together with Archbishop Cranmer, now acted as they would never have dared in the old King's time. Images, statues and vestments were thrown out of the churches, and the pictured walls were whitewashed over. The Latin Mass was abolished in favour of services in English, from a Prayer Book chiefly composed by Cranmer. The reformers judged the country by London and the sea-ports but, in the remoter areas, people were deeply offended by this overthrow of their old worship. Risings took place in the West country, where 10,000 men demanded a return to the religious laws of Henry VIII and were only silenced by the bullets of German mercenaries.

A gathering in Norfolk to grumble about Enclosures developed into a revolt led by *Robert Kett*, a tanner, whose forces held Mousehold Hill, outside Norwich,

ROBERT KETT LED A REVOLT IN NORFOLK

and refused the pardon offered by Somerset because they said they had done no wrong. Bloodshed ended the revolt, and blame for the disorders fell upon Somerset, who was removed by the Council to the Tower and later to the scaffold.

EDWARD VI WAS ONLY 10 YEARS OLD WHEN HE BECAME KING

NORTHUMBERLAND'S RULE

An able scoundrel who had become Duke of Northumberland, now took control of the country and of the young king, over whom he had great influence. Entirely selfish and without real religion, Northumberland supported the Protestants in order to grab what was left of Church property for himself and his supporters. The Catholic bishops were sent to the Tower and replaced by reformers like Hooper, Coverdale and Ridley, who helped Cranmer to publish a Second Prayer Book, more Protestant than the first.

Unhappily, the young king, who had already shown himself an ardent Protestant with the terrifying heartlessness of his father, was already dying. It became clear that the Catholic princess, Mary, daughter of Henry VIII and Catherine of Aragon, must succeed him.

At this point, Northumberland formed a desperate plan to save himself from a Catholic monarch.

LADY JANE GREY

Nearly forty years earlier, Henry VIII's younger sister had been made to marry Louis XII of France, when she was only a girl and he a widower over fifty ; in a year, her royal husband had died and she had married, this time for love, the Duke of Suffolk. It was the grandchild of that marriage, Jane Grey, a sweet child of sixteen, whose royal blood made her the victim of Northumberland's plot.

THE DUKE OF SOMERSET

Lady Jane was a Protestant, so Northumberland was able to persuade the sick young king that he must save his religion by setting aside Mary and Elizabeth, and bequeathing the crown to Lady Jane Grey. To make his own position safe, Northumberland arranged for his son, Lord Dudley, to marry her.

Lady Jane Grey proclaimed Queen

When Edward died, the innocent Lady Jane was proclaimed Queen, but Mary was warned of the plot just in time to ride from Hertfordshire to Norfolk, where she was sure of support. On the way, she boldly called on all loyal Englishmen to support her right to the throne, and they did so from admiration for her spirit, and because they knew that, as Henry's eldest child, she was the rightful Queen.

Mary enters London

Thus, on a wave of enthusiasm, Mary entered London, riding with her red-haired sister Elizabeth, whom the Londoners eyed with interest. Deserted by his own troops, Northumberland had no hope of escaping the end which he deserved, and, in keeping with his character, he wounded the Protestant cause by confessing that he had never been sincere. Lady Jane was kept in the Tower, where her pious gentleness could not save her from execution a year later.

THE CATHOLIC QUEEN

At her accession, Mary was thirty-seven. Years of sorrow and humiliation had given her a somewhat severe expression and, though naturally kind and brave, she lacked the glowing personality that might have carried through the policy on which her heart was set.

From the first, she was determined to restore the Catholic faith which had upheld her during the wrongs which she and her mother had suffered. She began cautiously, since the support of Parliament was needed to change the laws of the land. The Catholic

THE DUKE OF NORTHUMBERLAND

MARY ENTERED LONDON, RIDING WITH HER SISTER, ELIZABETH

bishops were let out of the Tower to make room for the leading Protestant clergy, including Cranmer, Latimer and Ridley. The old services in Latin, with all the ceremonies and vestments, were brought back, but Parliament jibbed at recognising the Pope, and would clearly refuse to restore the monastic lands.

WYATT'S REBELLION

It was Mary's marriage that destroyed her popularity, for she made up her mind to marry her cousin, Philip of Spain. She could not understand that Englishmen despised foreigners and hated the idea of their country becoming a small part of the huge Spanish empire.

MARY TUDOR

News of the match caused a number of risings, including a serious revolt in Kent under *Sir Thomas Wyatt*. The rebels approached London, whose citizens were only half-heartedly in support of the Queen, but her courage rallied them and the revolt petered out.

Queen Mary marries Philip of Spain

In 1554, Mary and Prince Philip were married in Winchester Cathedral, and, later that year, Cardinal Pole came from Rome to announce that the Pope had received England back into the Catholic Church. To Mary, it appeared that her position was secure enough to remove heresy from the kingdom. Parliament, it should be noted, now brought back the laws for burning heretics.

The first victims were Rogers, editor of " Mathew's Bible ", who was burnt alive at Smithfield, and Bishop Hooper, who died at Gloucester. By the end of the year, about seventy persons, young and old, important and humble, had died at the stake. They appeared to be defiant rather than penitent, and Latimer's words to Ridley, before the flames engulfed them, went through the land :

" Be of good comfort, Master Ridley, and play the man. We shall this day light such a candle, by God's grace, in England, as I trust shall never be put out."

Though the burnings seemed to encourage rather than stamp out heresy, there was no going back for Mary and Cardinal Pole. The arch-Protestant himself, Thomas Cranmer, must be made to repent. The smooth, gentle old man, who had steered out of so many troubles in the past, was brought to a state of mind in which he signed a confession denying the Protestant faith. He had still to die, and courage returned on the morning of his execution. Led out to repeat his confession, Cranmer denounced the Pope instead, and went to the stake, thrusting

SIR THOMAS WYATT WHO LED A REVOLT AGAINST THE QUEEN

first into the flames his hand that had signed the recantation.

The burnings went on and, from first to last, some 300 persons, mostly poor and ignorant folk, died. This was not a large number by Spanish standards, but the effect in England has never been forgotten.

Yet it is impossible not to pity Mary. She believed with all her heart that she was acting rightly for God and the true religion. In her marriage, she was deeply unhappy, for her hopes for a child were in vain. Her cold husband, who never returned her pathetic love, went home to become King of Spain and was soon to demand troops to help him against France. Calais, the last English possession, was lost, and the Queen, crushed by her unhappiness, died in November 1558.

Death of Mary

THE SETTLEMENT OF ELIZABETH

The news of Mary's death was carried by messenger to Hatfield Palace where Princess Elizabeth had been living in genteel captivity, since narrowly escaping a charge of treason after Wyatt's rebellion.

The young queen, Elizabeth

Elizabeth was twenty-five when she became Queen. Red-haired, with a thin curved nose, arched brows and glittering eyes, she had the Tudors' love of hunting, their skill in music and athletic sports, and her father's gift of majesty. She looked a queen and could speak like a monarch to Parliaments and foreign ambassadors, but, to her people, she was serenely cheerful, conversing easily with humble citizens, coarse watermen and sea-captains. For forty-five years she was to inspire love and obedience, yet she kept her own counsel, never trusted anyone completely nor revealed the secrets of her inmost mind. Thus, she was to preserve her crown and the independence of her kingdom.

BISHOP RIDLEY

Elizabeth had seen how persecution of Catholics in Edward VI's reign, and of Protestants under Mary, had led only to misery and national unrest. She sensed that most people would prefer a return to Henry VIII's religious policy and this, as far as possible, she aimed at, bearing in mind that the Protestants were on the increase and that oppression of her Catholic subjects would bring foreigners to their rescue.

The final break with Rome

The authority of the Pope was again abolished, and Parliament placed the monarch "over all persons and causes", making her "Governor", instead of "Supreme Head" of the Church, which amounted to the same thing, but caused less offence to Catholics. Services were to be in English, and Cranmer's Prayer Book, with some alterations, was brought back. Everyone was to attend church on Sundays, but the penalty for disobedience was no worse than a fine of one shilling.

Above all, there was to be no violent persecution to fan the faith of one side or the other. The Queen had no wish to probe deeply into beliefs, and men might pray as they pleased, so long as they did not try to challenge the official religion. Certainly, the Catholic bishops were removed, but they were not harshly treated. Some of the clergy resigned, but the vast majority accepted the changes quietly but without enthusiasm.

Catholic services undoubtedly went on in country houses, especially in the north, where Catholic priests attended many a death-bed, but most people went to their parish churches and became used to Cranmer's prayers and the English service. In the first eleven years of Elizabeth's reign, no Englishman was burned for his religion or executed for treason.

PART OF THE OLD PALACE, HATFIELD

THE KNOWN WORLD AT THE END OF THE FIFTEENTH CENTURY

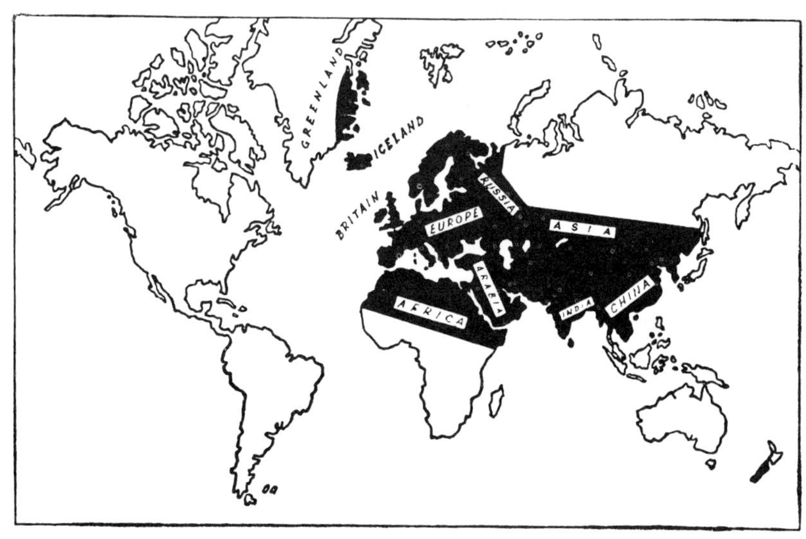

CHAPTER 5

THE WORLD ENLARGED

At the time when Henry Tudor was settling himself upon his newly won throne, most people had only the haziest idea of the extent of their own country, and there were few indeed who had any knowledge of the world outside Europe.

Marco Polo

Marco Polo's travels and the tall stories of adventurers had led folk to suppose that there were strange lands immensely far away to the east. These were generally known as the " Indies " and Cathay (China), where the great Khan ruled a fairy-tale empire, off whose coast lay the mysterious island of Cipango (Japan), and the longed-for Spice Islands. No man knew how far south stretched the continent of Africa, which, in any case, appeared to be an endless desert.

The ancient trade with the East still flowed along the caravan routes via Samarkand and Bagdad to Constantinople, to Azov on the Black Sea, to Aleppo in Asia Minor. Arab ships carried cargoes from India

A POCKET COMPASS AND SUNDIAL

CHRISTOPHER COLUMBUS

up the Red Sea to the markets of Alexandria, and from these ports and trading centres, the galleys of Genoa and Venice brought luxury goods to Europe —silks, carpets, sugar, perfume, cotton, figs, oranges and, above all, spices. On this trade, Genoa, Florence and Venice prospered magnificently, until the disaster of 1453, when the Ottoman Turks at last burst into Constantinople and were soon flooding into south-eastern Europe. Venice resisted, but trade became more and more uncertain, as the caravans were pillaged and the merchants were put to the sword.

PORTUGAL

Prince Henry the Navigator

Portugal, with her fine harbours, was better placed than Venice and Genoa for finding a new way to the east by sea. For years, Prince Henry of Portugal (1394–1460) had been urging his sailors to push farther down the coast of Africa, and he encouraged them to study navigation, now that the mariner's compass was in use, with the astrolabe for measuring the height of the sun to find latitude.

The Portuguese discovered the Canary Islands and the Azores, and, by 1445, their sailors had reached Cape Verde—the Green Cape. Here grass and trees were to be seen, instead of the African desert. Ivory, gold-dust and black slaves began to arrive in Lisbon from the Guinea coast and, in 1486, when *Bartholomew Diaz* rounded Africa's southernmost point, he could have sailed on to India but for the unwillingness of his homesick crew. King John II of Portugal told Diaz that his " Cape of Storms " must be renamed " The Cape of Good Hope ".

A MAP OF THE WORLD DRAWN BY DRISI IN THE TWELFTH CENTURY

SPAIN

The Moors were driven from Spain, and when the two largest states, Aragon and Castile, were united by the marriage of Ferdinand and Isabella, Spain came rapidly to greatness. A quarrel with Portugal led to Spain receiving the Canary Islands, while Portugal's right to the African trade was agreed. Spain must therefore find her own route to the opulent East.

Christopher Columbus

It was at this time that a Genoese sea-captain, named *Christopher Columbus*, who had settled in Lisbon as a chart-maker, was seeking help for a plan on which he had set his heart—no less than crossing the Atlantic Ocean to reach Asia. Columbus believed that Asia stretched much farther east than it really does, and that Cipango and the Chinese Empire were no great distance away for a navigator of skill and courage. He needed money and ships. The king of Portugal was engrossed in efforts to reach India by sailing round Africa, so Columbus tried his own city of Genoa, and sent his brother to sound Henry VII of England. While they hesitated, Queen Isabella of Spain promised to finance the voyage.

In August 1492, the expedition, consisting of the *Santa Maria* (100 tons) and the smaller *Nina* and *Pinta*, with combined crews of 120 men, sailed from Palos on the immortal voyage. After taking on food and water at the Canaries, the ships sailed westwards for thirty-three days and, as each day passed, Columbus drove on his timid, near-mutinous men, subduing them by his own faith, while he anxiously calculated his position in secret, concealing from the crew how far they had sailed.

Scraps of floating weed, a branch and a couple of birds kept hope alive, until, at 2 o'clock on Friday, the 12th October 1492, a look-out at the mast-head of the *Pinta* sighted land on the horizon. It was an

A LOOK-OUT IN THE "CROW'S NEST" SIGHTS LAND

island which Columbus named San Salvador, from which he sailed on to Cuba and other islands. These, he was convinced, lay near Japan on the fringe of Asia, so he called them the "West Indies". To the end of his life, he never realised that he had discovered a new continent, which was later named America, after Amerigo Vespucci, an explorer and writer.

THE POPE'S LINE

Spain and Portugal share the New World

Almost at once, with the approval of the Pope, Spain and Portugal took steps to divide the newly discovered world between themselves. All land west of a line 370 leagues from the Azores was to belong to Spain, all land to the east was Portugal's. Since South America had not yet been explored, neither side knew that the Pope's line ran through that continent, and this explains why Brazil became Portuguese while the rest of South America belonged to Spain. The agreement also explains why, later on, the Spaniards regarded English adventurers as trespassers on their private property.

THE PORTUGUESE REACH INDIA

The news of Columbus' triumph caused the Portuguese to redouble their efforts and, in 1497, eleven years after Diaz reached the Cape of Good Hope, King Emmanuel sent out an expedition headed by the *San Gabriel* under the command of a gentleman of the Court named *Vasco da Gama.*

The little fleet sailed to the Cape Verde islands, then far out into the Atlantic and southwards in a great curve until they sighted South Africa, after ninety-six days at sea, nearly three times as long as Columbus' voyage. Soon, the explorers found the crosses set up by Diaz, and on Christmas Day—the

TWO OF VASCO DA GAMA'S SHIPS

FERDINAND MAGELLAN

birthday or natal day of Christ—they lay off a new shore which da Gama called Natal. Sailing northwards, they met hostility from Arab ships engaged in trade with India, but a friendly prince lent them a pilot to guide the ships across the Arabian Sea to Calicut. On May 23rd 1498, after a voyage of almost a year, Vasco da Gama reached India.

The Portuguese were speedily repaid for their courage. Within a few years, they had arranged trade with princes and countries unknown to the rest of Europe.

Lisbon rapidly succeeded Venice as the greatest centre of trade with the East, but Portugal's separate might was not to last for long. In 1580, the country fell to Spain, and though she later regained her freedom, she never recovered the power of the first half of the sixteenth century.

MAGELLAN

How far south the Americas stretched and what lay beyond were unknown until *Ferdinand Magellan* made the most remarkable voyage in history. The great navigator was a Portuguese who had served in the East, but he went over to Charles V of Spain who welcomed him with the offer of a fleet of 5 ships. With these, he was to find a westerly route to the Spice Islands.

In 1519, Magellan sailed to America and then southwards, until forced to winter miserably ashore in the bleak land of Patagonia, where his crews came near to mutiny. One ship was lost, another turned back, but the rest sailed on, taking five weeks to battle through the strait named Magellan. When they came out into an ocean, it seemed so calm by contrast to the perils they had survived, that they called it the " Peaceful " or Pacific Ocean.

VASCO DA GAMA

Magellan believed he was now near the Spice Islands, but it took ninety-eight more days to reach the Philippines, a nightmare voyage during which the starving men were forced to eat rats, sawdust and leather. At last, they reached the islands where cinnamon, cloves, ginger and nutmegs grew. Here Magellan realised that he had joined up with the limit of eastern exploration. The world was not only proved to be round, but its size could now be checked. He had only to sail on to reach Portugal, but the commander who had survived so many dangers was killed in a fight on one of the islands. Without their captain, his men pushed on and, three years after they had set out, the eighteen men left alive sailed their battered ship into Seville. They were the first men who had sailed round the world.

SPANISH CONQUESTS

While Magellan was at sea, Spanish explorers probed into the new continent, showing less interest in North America than in the tropical regions of Central America. Here they came across an ancient empire ruled by the *Aztecs*, a strange people whose capital, Mexico, was so miraculously rich that the Spanish adventurers thought they had come to Paradise.

In 1519, a Spanish adventurer, *Hernando Cortes*, left Cuba to conquer the Aztecs, with a tiny force of 400 Spaniards and fifteen horses. They had firearms, however, and seven small cannons, as well as a leader of remorseless courage and greed.

The wild venture succeeded, partly because Cortes was superhuman in daring, and partly because the Aztecs regarded him as a god, whose coming had been long promised in legend.

MANY SHIPS WERE INFESTED BY RATS. MAGELLAN'S STARVING MEN WERE FORCED TO EAT THEM

A few years later, another Spaniard, *Francisco Pizarro*, discovered an even richer empire on the Pacific side of South America. It was the *Inca* Empire of Peru, which also collapsed when assaulted by a handful of white men whose courage and cunning were beyond belief.

Thus, on both sides of the Isthmus of Panama, Spain obtained wealth undreamed of by anyone in Europe. The settlers lived in arrogant splendour on plantations and in Spanish-style cities, which they forced the conquered peoples to build. Thousands of natives, called " Indians ", worked in the gold and silver mines of Peru and Mexico, while negroes from Africa laboured in the fields. Gold, silver and gems were brought by mule-train to the Isthmus, there to be loaded into the King's treasure ships which sailed for Spain, unchallenged and unmolested—at least for a time.

SPANISH WEALTH

Treasure from the New World

It is worth noting the effect of this dazzling wealth, for it will help us to understand why England was later to withstand the enmity of the richest empire on earth. Gold and silver poured across the Atlantic to Spain and, more gradually, into the markets of Europe, since much was spent on luxuries and on the hire of ships and soldiers. But treasure by itself is not wealth, for it cannot be eaten or used in any way, except for ornament. Since there was more gold about, prices went up and, strangest of all, the King of Spain was always desperately short of money. He was almost continuously at war with France and with the Turks ; he had to keep troops in his conquered lands and pay

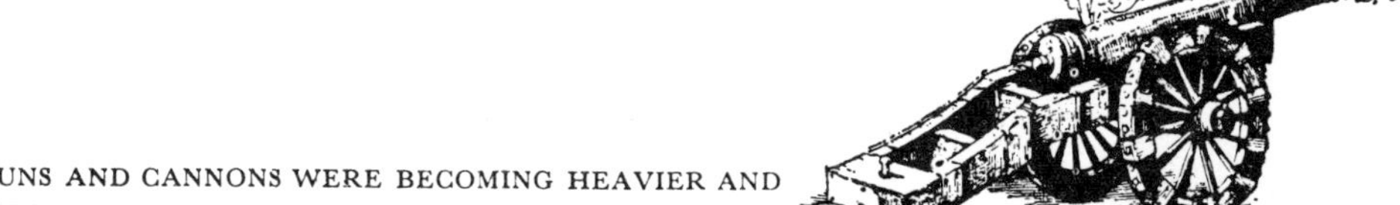

GUNS AND CANNONS WERE BECOMING HEAVIER AND WERE USED FOR LAND SIEGES AND SEA BATTLES

his way by borrowing at high rates of interest. The ship-loads of treasure somehow melted away through dishonesty, so that only a trickle of gold entered the royal coffers. Little money could be raised in Spain itself, because the clergy and nobles were not taxed and the ordinary people were too poor. Italy had been stripped well-nigh bare, and only from the Spanish Netherlands could real wealth be squeezed.

NEW FRANCE

While Spain and Portugal were gobbling up the riches of the newly discovered West and of the ancient East, the rest of Europe lagged behind in maritime enterprise. France looked not to the West, but to the chance of conquering a kingdom in northern Italy. Those French sailors who did reach the fringe of the New World, found, like the English, that they were poachers on Spain's private property. They made a living by picking up the scraps, trading when they could, selling slaves and turning to piracy.

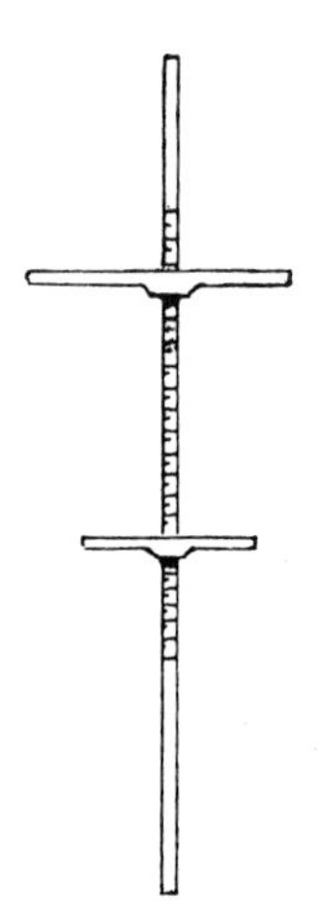

One notable voyage, however, was made by a French explorer, *Jacques Cartier*, who sailed along the coast of Canada and into the Gulf of St. Lawrence. In 1534, he set up a huge cross to claim the land for his King, as New France.

THE ENGLISH TAKE TO SEA-FARING

Compared with Spain and Portugal, and even with the fading power of Genoa and Venice, England was of small account, for her sea-faring had never amounted to much more than cross-Channel business in wool and wine, apart from coastal traffic and fishing.

Henry VII, in his money-making way, had realised that island prosperity must come from sea-borne trade, so he encouraged shipbuilding by giving relief

NAVIGATIONAL INSTRUMENTS OF THE FIFTEENTH CENTURY: A CROSS-STAFF, A COMPASS AND AN ASTROLABE

JOHN CABOT

from customs duties on goods carried in new ships. He also forbade foreign ships to load English goods when English ships were available, but he had to go warily for fear of offending the Hanse merchants. They controlled the goods on which all shipping depended. These were the " Baltic stores "—canvas, pitch for making seams water-tight, ropes, tar and long pines for making masts and spars. Without them, no ship could be built or kept at sea.

However, in Henry VII's reign, the first dry-dock was built at Portsmouth for refitting the royal fleet. Six new warships were built, with the *Regent* and *Sovereign* each over 700 tons.

Cabot sails to North America

At Bristol, the merchants were already looking westwards, having begun to trade with the Canaries and the Azores, and they kept representatives at Seville in Spain. It was from Bristol that *John Cabot* sailed on the first notable British voyage. Cabot, a Venetian who had settled in the city, was a skilled navigator who believed that Columbus had merely reached some outlying islands on the way to Cathay, so, with royal permission, he set out in 1497, only five years after Columbus. He took a more northerly course, expecting to reach the nearest point of Asia and then to sail along its coast to Cathay, Cipango and the Spice Islands. When he made landfall at Newfoundland, where he noticed the waters were teeming with cod, he was convinced that this was the tip of Asia, no great distance from warmer lands. Next year, he sailed again, with five ships equipped by Bristol and London merchants, but little is known about this voyage and the enterprise seems to have been written off as a trading failure.

HENRY VIII'S NAVY

More than his father, Henry VIII truly loved ships and all the pomp of a launching, when, attended by the whole Court, he would parade in a sailor's

SIR HUGH WILLOUGHBY

coat and trousers of gold cloth and actually take over the pilot's task. He was proud of his new dockyards at Woolwich and Deptford and of the school for pilots which he founded at Trinity House.

The King's Fleet grew in size until it totalled eighty-five ships. The noblest was *The Great Harry*, a monster of 1,500 tons, later replaced by another of the same name, smaller but more powerfully armed, with cannons that fired, not from the castles, but through ports in the sides. This English style of arming a ship to fire " broadsides " at the enemy was a great advance on the older way of fighting at sea, when ships rammed each other to enable the soldiers to get to grips.

THE FIRST SEA-DOGS

Tudor sea captains

For all Henry's interest in his fleet, the English still showed little taste for adventure. In 1521, for example, the King and Wolsey could not find merchants willing to risk money on another attempt to reach Cathay. However, in 1527, *John Rut* sailed to the north-west and then, baulked by ice, turned south to the West Indies, where the Spaniards fired on him when he attempted to trade. A year or two later, a Plymouth merchant, *William Hawkins*, commenced trading along the Guinea coast and even with Brazil, to bring home pepper, ivory and " brazilwood ", from which a dye was made.

In Edward VI's reign, a serious fall in cloth exports caused merchants to take more interest in ventures farther afield, and it is to the credit of the scoundrel Northumberland that he, ex-Lord Admiral, engaged old *Sebastian Cabot*, son of John, to advise on deep-sea navigation. Cabot recommended trade with the Barbary coast of Morocco, where sugar, dates and gum-arabic, used in cloth-finishing, could be exchanged for English goods. In Mary's reign, Thomas

Wyndham with a boy in his crew named *Martin Frobisher*, was trading along the African coast with negro chiefs for gold-dust and pepper, much to the indignation of the Portuguese.

It was Northumberland who sent out, in Edward VI's last year, the first expedition to Russia. *Sir Hugh Willoughby* was the commander of a little fleet which was to reach Asia by sailing north-east, for men believed that great rivers led into the heart of a fabulously rich continent and, at worst, there would be markets in the cold lands for English broadcloth. Willoughby and two of the ships were lost in the icy seas, but *Richard Chancellor* brought the third vessel into the White Sea to the port of Archangel, belonging to the Great Tsar of Russia, or Muscovy. Chancellor made a thousand-mile trip overland to Moscow, had audience with Tsar Ivan the Terrible and obtained trading rights for English merchants. On the way home from his second trip, Chancellor was drowned, but the *Muscovy Company* had been set up and the trade in furs, hides, rope, tallow and cloth prospered.

Chancellor reaches Russia

Thus, by the time Elizabeth came to the throne, a modest start had been made, though it was little enough compared with the triumphs of Portugal and Spain. Some humble trading and fishing, and a little business along the African coast had been achieved, but Henry VIII's navy had fallen into a sorry state, and the gold and spices, which all men coveted, belonged to empires too mighty to challenge.

" THE GREAT HARRY "

CHAPTER 6

THE REIGN OF ELIZABETH

THE NEW QUEEN

A WATCHMAN

THE people of England, even in the capital, had rarely seen the new Queen before her accession, for she had been kept out of sight during Mary's reign and, more than once, she had narrowly escaped the charge of treason.

Elizabeth was known to be a Protestant and a clever one, too. She was better educated than most men, and had no more difficulty with foreign languages and long-winded State papers than with the womanly arts of needlework, music and dancing. Men said she was like her father and had inherited his charm, as well as the Tudor determination to have her own way.

But if reports on the new queen were favourable, her chances of keeping the crown seemed uncommonly small.

THE DANGERS TO ENGLAND IN 1558

There was danger on every side. If Henry VIII's marriage to Anne Boleyn was not legal, then Elizabeth had no right to the throne and the true queen was Mary Queen of Scots, now living in France and married to the Dauphin, son of the French king. Catholics everywhere recognised Mary's right to the English crown. Meanwhile, Scotland was being held for her by French troops.

In France, an ambitious king, Henry II, had just recovered Calais, and was intent upon using his son's marriage to win control of both Scotland and England.

Philip of Spain naturally felt that he had first right

QUEEN ELIZABETH I

to the kingdom of his dead wife, so he offered to marry Elizabeth. She was well aware, however, that a Spanish marriage would be as disastrous for her as it had been for her sister. But if she refused him as husband, would he not come as conqueror?

At home, Elizabeth could not count on the loyalty of all her subjects. The North and the West country, as well as Ireland, were still Catholic in religion, yet Parliament and her counsellors wanted a Protestant policy that would invite rebellion and foreign invasion. If it came to war, England was no longer a tough nut to crack, for the Treasury was empty, the ships of her father's Navy were rotten or sold, the coastal defences in ruins and the militia of the shires unnumbered and untrained. Townsfolk and countrymen alike were discontented and religious bitterness divided the land.

ELIZABETH EVADES HER DIFFICULTIES

Luck and her early training came to Elizabeth's rescue. She realised that Philip of Spain, good Catholic as he was, would never allow the French king to put Mary Queen of Scots on England's throne, since, if France controlled the Channel, Philip was cut off from the Netherlands and his whole Empire threatened. So Elizabeth refused the offer of marriage, but allowed Philip to hope that her maidenly shyness might still be overcome. She engineered, as we have seen, a religious Settlement which did not satisfy the ardent Protestants but forced no one to revolt. She rightly judged that English Catholics, unless driven to despair, would prefer an English woman to a foreign queen.

The real menace, for the moment, was not Spain

but France, with its power to dominate Scotland. However, great changes took place there in the space of one year. The preaching of *John Knox* won over the Scottish people, except the Highlanders, to the burning Protestant religion of Calvin. In their horror of Catholic rule, the Scots were ready to overthrow the French alliance, and even to embrace their ancient enemy. A revolt against the French troops in Scotland was cautiously helped by Elizabeth, who sent soldiers and the best fleet she could muster. Fortunately, storms sank the French ships and drowned the troops that were on the way to rescue their countrymen.

Scotland sides with England

At this moment, Henry II of France died from an injury received in a tournament, and the Dauphin became King Francis II. His wife Mary was now Queen of France, Queen of Scotland and, she claimed, Queen of England, too. The danger to Elizabeth appeared to be worse than ever and she could only rely on Secretary Cecil to complete the downfall of French influence in Scotland, and hope for some miraculous relief.

It came within a year, for Francis II also died suddenly and Mary found herself no longer important or liked at the French Court. In 1561, she came home to her Scottish kingdom which she had not seen since babyhood. She was only nineteen, a beautiful, clever woman whose French upbringing made her

THE PREACHING OF JOHN KNOX WON OVER MANY SCOTTISH PEOPLE TO THE PROTESTANT RELIGION

a stranger to the manners and religious changes of her northern land, but if she played her cards well and married again wisely, she might yet become Queen of England, as well as of Scotland.

MARY QUEEN OF SCOTS

Mary chose disastrously, for she married her cousin Lord Darnley, a nobleman, who proved to be a worthless lout. He murdered her Italian secretary, Rizzio, almost before her eyes, and was himself murdered by the Earl of Bothwell, the Queen's new lover, another violent ruffian who " captured ", and then married her. These scandalous affairs so enraged the righteous Scots that they forced Mary from the throne, in favour of her infant son, James, and she fled to England.

Thus, by her own folly and misfortune, the glamorous Queen became a fugitive, appealing to her cousin Elizabeth for help, and asking to be recognised as heir to the English throne. As usual, Elizabeth gave no definite answer, wishing to keep the Catholics quiet while she held their trump card, and anxious to avoid angering her Protestant subjects. Mary was kept, half-guest, half-prisoner, in various northern castles, where the hapless woman busied herself ceaselessly with plots and letters, which did not escape the watchful eyes of Cecil and the Protestant master-spy, Walsingham.

With Mary in safe-keeping and Scotland in Protestant hands, there was much less danger from France, where a savage struggle developed between Catholics and Huguenots (Protestants). English sympathy was with the Huguenots, but even the horror of St. Bartholomew's Eve (1572), when thousands of Huguenots were butchered in the streets of Paris, did not shock Elizabeth into acting rashly. She kept up

The massacre of St. Bartholomew's Eve

an uneasy peace with France, allowing negotiations to drag on for a marriage with first one, and then another French prince. Meanwhile, she quietly sent just enough help to the Huguenots to keep the struggle alive, so that England was left alone.

ENGLAND AND SPAIN

Since the burning aim of Philip II's existence was to wipe out the heresy of Protestantism, he could not look kindly upon Elizabeth's religious Settlement nor upon her help to the Scottish Calvinists. But, as long as Elizabeth was fending off the French menace, he was prepared to put up with a good deal that displeased him. He fully intended to bring the disobedient island back to the true religion as soon as he found time to attend to the matter.

For the moment, Philip had problems even greater than England for, in the Netherlands, the industrious burghers had never ceased plaguing him for self-government, and they clung obstinately to their Protestant religion. In 1567, Philip sent the Duke of Alva with 12,000 hard-bitten Spanish troops to wipe out heresy by a reign of terror, in which thousands of Netherlanders died and many fled to England. William of Orange, known as " William the Silent ", placed himself at the head of the heroic rebels, whom Cecil and Walsingham tried to help by persuading the Queen to send troops and ships.

Elizabeth, as ever, acted cautiously. She had a natural dislike of aiding rebels against their lawful ruler, besides a healthy desire to avoid war with Spain. So she sent " underhand " support to the Netherlands, allowed the Sea-Beggars (Dutch privateers who attacked Spanish shipping) to use English ports, and turned a blind eye to the piratical exploits of her own sea-captains.

THE MARRIAGE GAME

For a good many years now, there had been no feeling in England that the Queen should rule alone. On the contrary, England had not liked its recent experience of rule by a Queen, in an age when men were the masters and women considered fit only for child-bearing. Cecil, the Council and Parliament constantly reminded Elizabeth of her duty to marry and provide England with a son and heir of the Protestant faith.

Elizabeth kept her own secrets, and we shall never know the real reasons why she did not marry.

The truth probably is that she realised more clearly than her ministers that the greatest safety for herself and the kingdom lay in remaining single. The hand of England's Queen was a prize which kept Spain and France on tenterhooks and, as the suitors came and went—Philip II, the Earl of Arran, the Earl of Leicester, Archduke Charles, the Prince of Sweden, the Dukes of Anjou and Alençon—Elizabeth accepted their gifts and elaborate wooing with all the

ELIZABETH EXPECTED DEVOTION AND DEMANDED FLATTERY FROM HER COURTIERS

The character of the Queen

delight of a vain woman playing an intricate game. She expected devotion and demanded flattery from the crowd of handsome courtiers whom she kept fluttering about her, teasing and flirting with them to the despair of her serious-minded counsellors. Even when she was an old woman, she was still behaving like a coy schoolgirl, with a French prince so ugly that she called him her " Frog ", but, for all her vanity, she never lost her head or failed to remember that *any* marriage would invite disaster.

A foreign husband would have been unpopular ; a Catholic would cause the Protestants to revolt ; a Protestant would bring Catholic aid to Mary Queen of Scots ; a French prince would provoke war with Spain, and an English lord, even her dear Leicester, would rouse the rest to jealousy. But as long as all could hope, none would dare to offend her, and she could keep her power to herself.

THE SEA-DOGS

The tales of sailors who came into Bristol, Portsmouth and Thames-side awoke in Englishmen a thirst for riches and an ambition to sail as far as any foreigner. Early in Elizabeth's reign, the Portuguese ambassador was complaining that the English ships were trading along the coast of West Africa, to which the Queen replied that they must cease the traffic—but she did nothing to make them obey.

In the Channel, many an English lad learned his trade by helping to capture and rob Spanish vessels on their way to the Netherlands. There were Englishmen with the French Huguenots when they sallied out from their stronghold La Rochelle, and others with the Sea-Beggars, who put into Dover to sell their spoils.

EVEN WHEN ELIZABETH WAS AN OLD WOMAN, SHE STILL BEHAVED LIKE A COY SCHOOLGIRL

West-country gentlemen and sea-captains, like Martin Frobisher and William Hawkins, Mayor of Plymouth, had ships cruising in the Channel to rob the Spaniards and bring their cargoes into Plymouth and Southampton. From the profits, Hawkins built a private fleet of sixteen well-armed ships which, as a trusted, loyal subject, he put to the Queen's service whenever she needed them.

MANY OF THE SHIPS USED BY THE ENGLISH SEAMEN WERE OF LESS THAN 20 TONS

ENGLISH SEAMEN IN THE NEW WORLD

While the Channel privateers were reaping a harvest, *John Hawkins*, brother of the Mayor and son of William who had started the Guinea trade, was operating on more distant seas. He sailed to the African coast, where he bought or captured negroes, and took them across the Atlantic to sell them at a good profit, along with English goods, to the planters in the Spanish possessions.

Hawkins in the Caribbean

On his third voyage to the Caribbean, Hawkins traded successfully along the Spanish Main and was on his way home with the profits safely aboard, when a severe gale forced him to enter the Spanish port of *San Juan de Ulua*, in the Gulf of Mexico. In accordance with the rules of the game, Hawkins took possession of the port, promising to behave peaceably, while he repaired his flag ship, the *Jesus of Lubeck*, which, with the *Minion*, belonged to the Queen. Before the work was completed, however, a Spanish fleet appeared which Hawkins could have kept out of the port. Since England and Spain were officially at peace, he decided to allow it to enter, explaining

JOHN HAWKINS

the arrangement to the Viceroy of New Spain on board, who promised friendship and help.

Three days later, the Spaniards made a sudden attack, killing many of the English and taking all their ships, except the *Minion*, in which Hawkins escaped, and the *Judith*, commanded by a youngster named Francis Drake. Drake, like his leader, fought his way out with tigerish ferocity. The two vessels, damaged and without stores, made a terrible voyage home, and when the *Minion* neared land, the fifteen men still alive in Hawkins's ship were too weak to bring her into Plymouth.

The Spaniards doubtless considered themselves justified in outwitting their King's enemies, but in England, the story of the black treachery of San Juan spread from port to port, and there were many, besides Drake, who swore to take revenge. If the Spaniards would not allow honest trade, they must put up with piracy.

FRANCIS DRAKE

San Juan, and lesser incidents of the same kind, led to undeclared war in the Caribbean. A host of British and Huguenot privateers, mostly small craft, cruised along the Spanish Main, robbing ships, plundering settlements and, when strong forces hunted them, disappearing into the creeks and inlets of the tropical coast.

Drake became the " master thief " of this company, for his courage and astounding energy, his ability to plan attacks and carry them out with relentless drive, raised him above the petty marauders.

On one expedition, during which he won the devoted help of the Cimaroons (bands of escaped slaves living in the swamps and forests), Drake landed on the Isthmus and captured the mule-train of gold from

MULE-TRAINS CARRIED THE GOLD TO THE COAST

Panama. His greatest exploit was to sail round South America into the Pacific to rob the astonished Spaniards on their private ocean. He claimed California for the Queen as New Albion, and brought the *Golden Hind* right across the world, through the East Indies, where tons of spices were added to the gold below decks, and round the Cape into Plymouth Sound.

This voyage (1577–80), the greatest yet made by English sailors, lasted three years. Drake, who had taken treasure worth twice the royal income, must have waited anxiously for the Queen's pleasure to be known. If peace had been made in his absence, he could expect a pirate's end, but when Elizabeth knighted him on his own deck, war with Spain moved a long step nearer.

ENGLISH SEAMEN

Attempts to find a North-West passage

Men still believed that China could be reached by a northerly route. Willoughby had perished in that hope, and Chancellor had set up the Muscovy trade in furs and tallow, while seeking the spices and silks of the East. The Cabots had been convinced that a North-West passage to Asia lay beyond the icy coasts of North America which the Spaniards disdained.

Martin Frobisher, an experienced seaman, was brought to the Queen's notice by Sir Humphrey Gilbert, himself a sailor and a soldier too. In the year 1576, Frobisher explored the coast of Greenland and northern Canada, and returned believing he had found the Passage. Next year, he sailed again and brought back some black stones which seemed to contain veins of gold.

The search for gold

When news of these stones reached London, there was great excitement at the prospect of England having treasure of her own, and Frobisher departed a third time, with a fleet of 15 ships, while plans were started to build furnaces to smelt the precious ore. The project collapsed when tons of black stone proved to be worthless. Frobisher was temporarily under a cloud, though he was later to serve with Drake in the West Indies and to command a ship against the Armada.

Frobisher's voyages fired *John Davis* to penetrate further into the icy seas but, though he made important discoveries and can be regarded as the father of Arctic exploration, the North-West Passage eluded him, as it defeated poor *Henry Hudson*, set adrift by his own men in the next reign.

All this time, English seamen were gaining knowledge and confidence. Men of influence at Court, like the Earl of Warwick, Sir Humphrey Gilbert and Walter Raleigh, encouraged the sea-dogs and supported their voyages, when they were not adventuring on their own account. The Queen liked to meet her sea-captains, to hear what was afoot and to take a share in the risks and profits, so long as she did not provoke Spain too far. *Sir Richard Grenville*, one of the swashbuckling gentry of Devon, had a scheme to explore the Southern Seas and find the unknown continent, Terra Australis Incognita; *Humphrey Gilbert* took a party to found a colony in Newfoundland which he annexed for the Crown. The scheme failed for the time being, but the idea of colonies for English people lived on, like the story of Gilbert's death, when, in mountainous seas on the way home, he was last seen from another vessel, sitting on the deck of the *Squirrel*, "with a book in his hand, crying out to us . . . 'We are as near to Heaven by sea as by land.'"

MARTIN FROBISHER

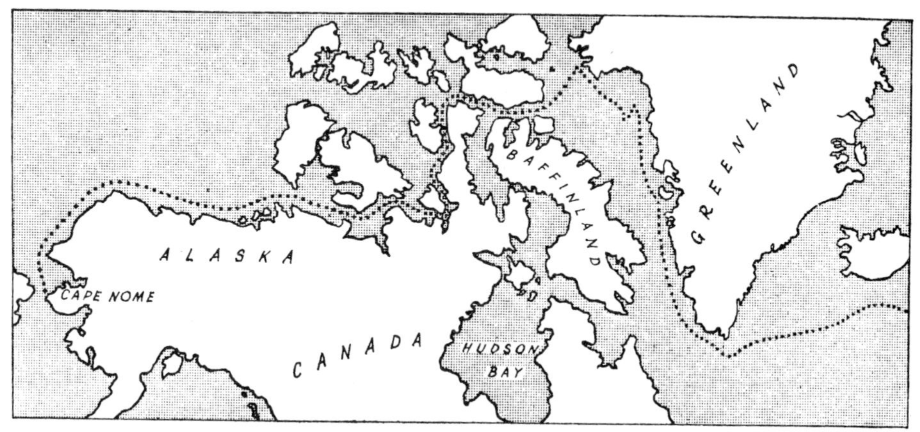

MANY ATTEMPTS WERE MADE TO FIND A NORTH-WEST PASSAGE ROUND NORTH AMERICA TO CHINA *Scale : 1 in.=1,000 miles*

Many a vessel of no more than 15 or 20 tons was built in the yards of sea-towns like Bideford and Brixham, fitted out and victualled by moneyed townsmen, and manned by local men, under a captain who had sailed perhaps with Hawkins. They made for the recognised freebooters' area between the Spanish Main and the Isthmus of Panama, where they joined the craft already at work, hunting down Spanish vessels and banding together to attack larger galleons. If they met opposition, they fought not only with firearms, but with swords, knives, bows and arrows. When the Spaniard surrendered, they took the money, plate and useful stores to feed themselves, and let him go, unless they needed his ship to replace their own. It was a risky trade, for not more than half the crew would see Devon again. Some would die of wounds, some in Spanish prisons or under the Inquisition's torture, and more from disease that attacked every ship's crew. At the end of the voyage, the profits were shared out according to the rules for " adventuring on thirds "—one third to the owners of the ship, one third to those who fitted her out and one third to the crew, who doubtless took some private booty as well.

" Adventuring on thirds "

WAR WITH SPAIN: THE RISING OF THE NORTHERN EARLS

Elizabeth, as we have seen, did not greatly care about men's religion so long as they were loyal, but the existence of Mary Queen of Scots was a strain on the loyalty of the Catholics in the north. Plots were constantly afoot and, in 1569, there was a rising of the Roman Catholic earls of Northumberland and Westmorland. The rebel force was dispersed without difficulty, after which Elizabeth dealt out punishment that was savage, even by her father's standards.

THE EXECUTION OF MARY QUEEN OF SCOTS

Plots against Elizabeth

Next year, by excommunicating Elizabeth, the Pope made it the duty of Catholics to dethrone her. Fresh plots were hatched to assassinate Elizabeth and bring over a Spanish army to take the crown for Mary. The Pope and the Spanish ambassador encouraged the plotters whose leader was the Duke of Norfolk, but Cecil and Walsingham scented them out through keeping watch on their agent, *Ridolfi*, an Italian banker living in London. This time, the Duke of Norfolk was beheaded.

Parliament, by now well and truly frightened, increased the penalties for avoiding church services. For the first time in Elizabeth's reign, Catholics began to suffer persecution, and even death—not, it was held, for their religion, but for treachery. The Pope replied by setting up colleges abroad to train English youths as Jesuit priests, who came secretly into the country to win converts for the Catholic faith.

When Cecil, now Lord Burghley, unearthed yet another plot, Elizabeth refused to act against her royal cousin, but three years later, letters were intercepted between a conspirator named *Babington* and Mary herself. These letters proved that she was

LETTERS WERE FOUND WHICH PROVED THAT MARY WAS STILL PLOTTING A FOREIGN INVASION

still plotting a foreign invasion and the removal of Elizabeth. Parliament, Burghley and Walsingham demanded execution and, at long last, the Queen brought herself to sign the death warrant. Two days later (1587), Mary Queen of Scots met her death with brave dignity, in the hall of Fotheringay Castle :

> " Her prayers being ended, the executioners, kneeling, desired Her Grace to forgive them her death : who answered ' I forgive you with all my heart, for now I hope you shall make an end of all my troubles.' . . .
>
> " Then the two women departed from her, and she kneeling down upon the cushion most resolutely and without any token or fear of death, she spake aloud a Psalm in Latin . . . then lying on the block most quietly and stretching out her arms cried ' In manus tuas, Domine. ' " (Into Thy hands, Lord.)

Execution of Mary Queen of Scots

It was now certain that Philip would act, for the dead Queen had left her claim to the English throne, not to her son, but to Philip himself.

A SEAMAN

Events at last seemed to have turned in Philip's favour, for his ability to make war had been vastly improved by seizing Portugal in 1580, with all her wealth, harbours and navy. In the Netherlands, the Duke of Parma was making better progress than Alva ; William of Orange had been murdered, and Elizabeth's force of 6,000 men under Leicester had met with little success. Agents reported that the Catholics in England would rise in support of a Spanish invasion.

THE ARMADA

Philip's plan was for Parma to cross the narrow seas and land in southern England, with an army of crack troops, better-armed and more experienced than any that Elizabeth could raise. To hold the Channel and keep the Netherlands in check, a large fleet, or *Armada*, would bring 20,000 troops from Spain.

Philip of Spain prepares his Armada

Crippled, as always, by debts and difficulties, Philip put his shipyards to work, acquired Italian, German and Flemish vessels of various sizes for troop transports, scoured the Mediterranean for sailors, and steadily amassed the stores, food, gunpowder, shot and armour that were needed for the great invasion. In Flanders, the Duke of Parma built hundreds of flat-bottomed craft to carry horses and men which were to be conveyed along specially dug canals to Dunkirk and Nieuport.

News of these immense preparations could not be kept secret from Walsingham's spies. In England, men began to look to their weapons, to practise their drill on the greens and to keep the warning beacons ready. With the Queen's permission, half-hearted, because she hoped that peace might still be patched up, Francis Drake took twenty-four ships into Cadiz harbour, defying its fortress guns and armed galleys,

AN ADMIRAL

to capture or destroy thirty-seven warships, many smaller vessels and vast quantities of stores. This famous "singeing of the King of Spain's beard" delayed the Armada for a year, but did not weaken Philip's determination. His best admiral died and he had to give the command to the Duke of Medina Sidonia, a loyal gentleman who did not want the task and knew he was unfitted to carry it out.

The Armada sails

At last, in 1588, the Armada sailed from Lisbon, 130 strong, of which about forty were warships, the largest known as galleasses, and the rest merchantmen and small craft filled with troops. The great fleet slowly approached the English Channel and formed up in line abreast, the warships guarding the transports, to make stately progress at about two miles an hour towards the Flemish coast. Philip had forbidden attacks on English ports, such as Plymouth, for the prime object was to join forces with the Duke of Parma's army.

Unknown to the Spaniards, the main English fleet had moved to Plymouth. Lord Seymour was in the Downs, with a small force ready to assist the Dutch ships that were watching the coast for any movement of Parma's barges. The English navy amounted to no more than thirty-six royal warships and these were none too well supplied, but as many as 150 armed merchantmen of various sizes, equipped and manned by coastal towns, were ready to join the fleet, all more or less under the command of Lord Howard of Effingham, an able and experienced sailor.

On July 19th, the Armada was sighted and the English captains, taken by surprise, had difficulty in getting to sea, since the wind that brought the enemy up-Channel hindered ships trying to leave Plymouth.

A NAVAL GUNNER HOLDING A RAMROD

By the 21st, they were ready to attack, while, ashore, beacons and drums had roused the country to face the danger which Elizabeth and Cecil had fended off for thirty years.

Howard's four squadrons, under Drake (the vice-admiral), Hawkins, Frobisher and himself, skirted the slow-moving Armada to fire broadsides and cripple individual ships, which could be captured when they fell behind the fleet. These tactics were fairly successful, but the Spaniards were stronger than even Drake had reckoned, and their guns more powerful than any he had known before. Though one or two "great ships" were crippled, many damaged, and much execution done among the soldiers on deck, the Armada held its course and was able to anchor off Calais on the 27th. So far, Medina Sidonia had carried out his task. The English had never got within decisive range, and it only remained for him to make contact with Parma.

Thus, when Seymour and old Winter joined Howard at anchor a mile to the windward of the Spaniards, the situation was critical for England. A week at sea and much firing had brought food and ammunition very low—"Sir," Howard wrote to Walsingham, on only the second day out, "for the love of God and our country, let us have with some speed some great shot sent us of all bigness . . . and some powder with it."

The enemy fleet had to be broken up and, at this point, the ancient device of fireships achieved what seamanship and gunnery had failed to do.

In the night, eight old merchant-ships were towed towards the enemy, set ablaze and left to drift with tide and wind into the close-anchored fleet. As the blazing ships approached, with gunpowder already exploding, panic seized the Armada. To the sailors' dread of fire at sea were added

A MEDAL WAS STRUCK TO COMMEMORATE THE DEFEAT OF THE ARMADA

the confusion of darkness and ignorance of the coastal waters. Cables were cut and every ship made out of the anchorage as best it could.

The Armada defeated

Dawn saw the great fleet scattered along the low-lying coast, some aground, some returning, and all without orders. The English squadrons attacked all day, and kept at it until the last of their shot had gone, and this battle, known as *Gravelines*, so damaged the Spanish warships that invasion was out of the question.

All that remained to Medina Sidonia was to save his fleet for another day. But escape was not easy, for Parma had not secured a friendly port to shelter damaged ships, and a south-west gale prevented return down the Channel. So, dogged by Howard as far as the Firth of Forth, the tattered Armada fled northwards to sail round Britain. Storms drove some ships to Norway and more on to the rocky shores of Scotland and Ireland where the unruly inhabitants completed the destruction begun by English guns and heavy seas.

Out of 130 ships more than half were lost with two-thirds of the troops—over 2,000 corpses were washed up in one Irish bay alone—with all their armour, guns, priests and crucifixes. Only fifty-three battered vessels reached Spain. Medina Sidonia was reviled by all, except his king, who accepted the disaster with splendid dignity. " I sent you out," he said, " to war with men and not with the elements." Then, with dauntless obstinacy, he turned to repair the damage and to renew the war, for he had never a thought of giving up the struggle which to him was a religious duty.

England breathed a sigh of proud and astonished relief, for none had under-rated the danger, and the commanders knew that, well as they had

MANY SPANISH SHIPS WERE WRECKED ON THE ROCKY SHORES OF IRELAND AND SCOTLAND

fought, the weather had been on their side. The words on Elizabeth's medal, " God blew and they were scattered ", expressed the country's feeling that Heaven had saved the Protestant cause.

AFTER THE ARMADA

For the time being, England was safe, but Spain remained immensely strong, so plans were made to follow up the victory with another blow. Hawkins wanted to keep a fleet at sea between the Azores and Spain to intercept the treasure-ships, but Drake's plan to destroy the remnants of the Armada and to set Don Antonio on the throne of Portugal found favour instead.

1589 saw the unsuccessful attack on Corunna and the failure to take Lisbon, which dealt a blow to Drake's renown and, worse, blinded the Queen to the fact that her best—and cheapest—weapon was the Fleet. Like the Spaniards and almost everyone else, she still believed that wars were won by soldiers and that ships were merely for coastal defence. In the fifteen years following the Armada, she spent only half a million pounds on the Navy, but somehow found three millions for land forces which achieved next to nothing.

From time to time, expeditions under Hawkins, Frobisher, Howard and Grenville went out to raid the Spaniards, but Hawkins' plan of a blockade was never taken up, so the treasure-ships got through, helped by Philip's new tactics of using fast well-armed vessels which sailed at irregular intervals. As the Spanish fleet recovered its strength, the English answer, unbelievably, was to send fewer ships to sea. In the Netherlands, in France and Ireland, however, English armies were fighting at great cost and with little result.

Before the Armada, fear of Spain had created a

SIR WALTER RALEIGH BROUGHT POTATOES AND THE HABIT OF SMOKING BACK FROM AMERICA

body of daring seamen, who were backed by a proud, determined Queen, but the danger receded as they grew older, and there was none to replace them. Grenville died of wounds in the last fight of the *Revenge*, and Frobisher was mortally wounded when leading a flotilla against a Spanish stronghold in Britanny. Drake and Hawkins died at sea during their last raid on the West Indies (1596), when nothing went well, for the Spaniards were better prepared than in the old days.

Cadiz is captured

In the same year, 1596, when another Armada was known to be preparing, Howard, Raleigh, and the Queen's young favourite, Essex, took part in the greatest triumph since 1588. They captured *Cadiz* and destroyed the town and shipping, though Elizabeth grumbled that the amount of booty was small. After this, the war gradually petered out, as Philip grew old and his best general, Parma, died.

RALEIGH

After Sir Humphrey Gilbert's death at sea, his right to make settlements in distant lands fell to his half-brother, Walter Raleigh, the brilliant, arrogant favourite of the Queen. Unable to obtain her permission to leave the Court, Raleigh sent out colonists under Grenville to a warmer coast than Newfoundland, which he named *Virginia*, after the Queen. The survivors of this party were brought home by Drake. Another batch perished, probably through quarrels and a hopeless search for gold. A third party met the same fate and Raleigh lost a fortune, because men still looked to the New World for easy treasure, and not yet for homes and farms. After questioning seamen and sending out an expedition, Raleigh himself went to Guiana in Central America to travel up the Orinoco and make a treaty with the natives.

He believed that the country was fabulously rich, and that its capital, Manoa, the " El Dorado " or City of Gold, lay within reach. Raleigh came home with his dream, but was prevented from returning, until his last tragic expedition in James I's reign.

WEAPONS OF THE SIXTEENTH CENTURY

ENGLISH VENTURES

Besides these romantic schemes and private cruises to the West Indies, there were many attempts to establish respectable trade. The Levant or Turkey Company was trading in the eastern Mediterranean ; *Thomas Cavendish*, in 1586–88, followed Drake's route round the world, but died on his next voyage with *John Davis*, the Arctic explorer. Their experiences of the terrifying Magellan Straits and the strength of the Spaniards in their private Pacific Ocean caused London merchants to prefer ventures which took the easier route round the Cape to the East Indies, where the object was to rob the Portuguese and learn the Eastern trade.

Almost at the end of her reign, in 1600, the Queen granted a charter to the *East India Company* and, next year, the first of the Company's expeditions, commanded by *John Lancaster*, with Davis as his chief pilot, rounded Africa and sailed to India and Java.

REBELLION IN IRELAND

Since Henry VII's reign, the Tudors had never lost sight of the need to bring Ireland under their rule, for the poverty-stricken country with its unruly chiefs, private wars and Catholic religion, made it a happy hunting-ground for any who would defy England or plan an invasion. The Pope and Philip were constantly stirring up trouble there, much as Elizabeth interfered in the Netherlands. To subdue the troublesome inhabitants, English gentry were given grants of land confiscated from the Irish.

Troubles in Ireland

Repeated risings and massacres took place. Spanish and Italian soldiers came and went, and though some of the English, like Raleigh and the poet Spenser, made attempts to settle their Irish estates, most of those who received grants of land were intent only on squeezing money from them. The desperate Irish found a real leader in *Hugh O'Neal, Earl of Tyrone.* This master of irregular warfare so rattled the English that the dashing *Earl of Essex* had to be sent out in 1599, as Lord Lieutenant, but he made a sad mess of the campaign against Tyrone, and could do no more than obtain a truce.

The testy old Queen was furious at the waste of money, for she had spent heavily on the army. Essex, brave and foolish, rushed home to confront the enemies at Court who were poisoning the Queen's mind against him. Dusty and bedraggled from the journey, but confident of his power to charm, he burst into the royal apartments, but was coldly dismissed for his impertinence. Disgrace so enraged Essex that he behaved like a naughty child, gathering desperate men about him and indulging in wild plans to overthrow the Council. His arrest and execution for treason followed, for, though Elizabeth had doted on the wilful, gifted youth, she could not forgive a rebellious nobleman.

ESSEX BURST INTO THE ROYAL APARTMENTS BUT WAS COLDLY DISMISSED FOR HIS IMPERTINENCE

THE GREAT QUEEN

Lord Mountjoy succeeded in subduing the Irish rising, but at home the Queen seemed to have lost the will to live much longer. She was nearly seventy, a great age which no English monarch had ever reached. Nearly all those who had served her gloriously in the perilous years had gone—Leicester, Walsingham, Burghley, Drake and her sea-dogs. Even her old enemy, Philip, was dead, and now the last of her favourites, young Essex. The sparkle of her reign and the relish for ruling in the midst of dangers had faded, and, more from a weary sense that her day was over than from illness, she turned towards death.

The death of Queen Elizabeth

A year earlier, she had summoned the Commons for the last time and, though she still would not discuss her successor, everyone knew it must be James VI of Scotland, her cousin's son. In her most regal way, she cancelled some of the more hateful Monopolies,* and made her farewell speech to the Members and to England, saying,

> " I count the glory of my crown that I have reigned with your loves . . . and though you have had, and may have, many mightier and wiser princes sitting in this seat, yet you never had, nor shall have, any that will love you better."

* A monopoly was the sole right to make or to import an article (e.g. vinegar, spices). This right was given to a courtier or sold to a merchant who could then charge whatever price he pleased.

A TUDOR CARRIAGE

CHAPTER 7

ELIZABETH'S ENGLAND

TOWN AND COUNTRY

A COUNTRYWOMAN GOING TO MARKET

In the England of Queen Elizabeth I, the total population was between four and five millions, of whom the greater part lived south of Nottingham, for the only town in the North that could rival Bristol, Exeter or Ipswich was York. The forests, big as they were, had thinned, especially in East Anglia, so that the government and shipbuilders were already concerned about the rate of tree-felling and the scarcity of good timber.

Farming in Elizabethan times

In many parts, the huge open fields were still cultivated in strips and patches, for Enclosures * (fields fenced or hedged), were mostly found in the Midlands, where the biggest flocks of sheep were kept, with hedgerows to stop them straying. However, sheep were everywhere in every part of the country, for English wool and English cloth were still the chief money-makers.

Around London, and especially in Kent and in Essex, were market gardens, orchards and the new hop-fields ; the cornlands were mostly in the East, but barley and rye grew in every parish to provide its ale and bread. The Fens, a great area round Ely, were undrained swamp, peopled only by the fen-men who fished, and even farmed, on stilts. In Wales and the North, were vast stretches of heath and moor, almost uninhabited, and on the Scottish border, feudal tribes lived by rough farming and thieving, answering only to their own earls, who were petty kings until Elizabeth put them down.

* See note overleaf.

IN THE FENS MEN FISHED, AND EVEN FARMED, ON STILTS

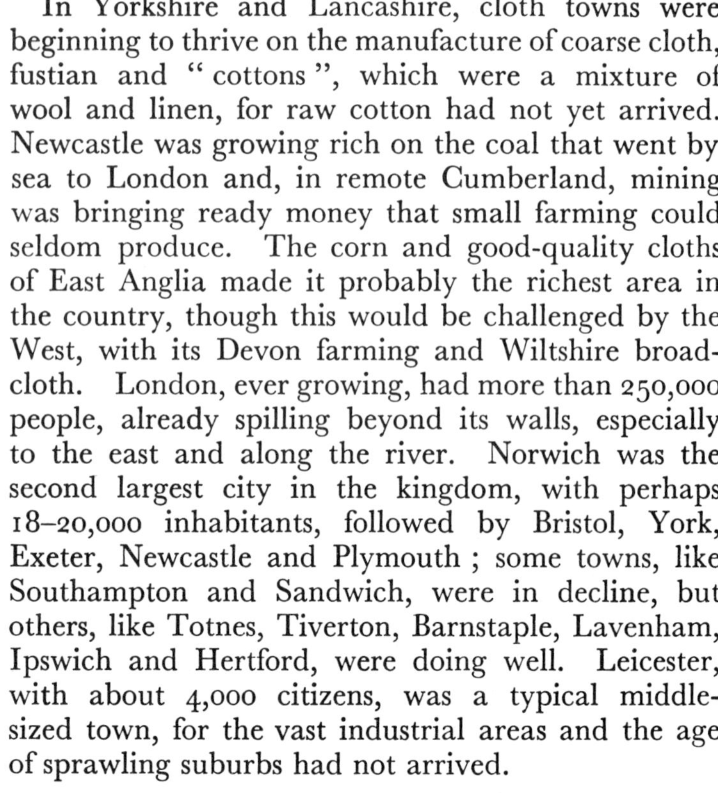

New industries

In Yorkshire and Lancashire, cloth towns were beginning to thrive on the manufacture of coarse cloth, fustian and "cottons", which were a mixture of wool and linen, for raw cotton had not yet arrived. Newcastle was growing rich on the coal that went by sea to London and, in remote Cumberland, mining was bringing ready money that small farming could seldom produce. The corn and good-quality cloths of East Anglia made it probably the richest area in the country, though this would be challenged by the West, with its Devon farming and Wiltshire broadcloth. London, ever growing, had more than 250,000 people, already spilling beyond its walls, especially to the east and along the river. Norwich was the second largest city in the kingdom, with perhaps 18–20,000 inhabitants, followed by Bristol, York, Exeter, Newcastle and Plymouth ; some towns, like Southampton and Sandwich, were in decline, but others, like Totnes, Tiverton, Barnstaple, Lavenham, Ipswich and Hertford, were doing well. Leicester, with about 4,000 citizens, was a typical middle-sized town, for the vast industrial areas and the age of sprawling suburbs had not arrived.

THE PEOPLE

Most of the people, probably four-fifths, lived in the country, that is to say in their hamlets and villages, though these were often called "towns". They

* Enclosures. The practice of enclosing land with hedges or fences had been going on since the Middle Ages, but was particularly common in Tudor times. It declined in the seventeenth century, but increased again in the eighteenth. Rich men bought or acquired strips of land to make larger fields ; they also fenced in common-land and woods. Thus, large numbers of sheep could be kept and more efficient ways of farming could be developed, but fewer men were needed on the land. The poor suffered unemployment and the loss of their grazing rights. They grumbled bitterly about Enclosures, which they often blamed for all their troubles. Elizabeth tried to check Enclosures, but the practice made for better agriculture in the long run.

TWO SERVANTS

AN ELIZABETHAN COUNTRY HOUSE

were tougher and noisier than we are, quicker to laugh and sing, to quarrel and strike blows. Reckless and boastful, they were still absurdly fearful of witchcraft and strangely respectful of high rank. As obstinate and argumentative as children, they were indeed young people, married at 14 or 16, middle-aged at 30 and seldom likely to live as long as the Queen or Burghley.

The nobles now had less power and were fewer in number than for centuries—the Wars of the Roses and the first two Tudors had seen to that—and though they kept up great households and vied with each other in the magnificence with which they entertained the Queen, they no longer had the wealth or retainers to threaten the Crown. The Rebellion of the Northern Earls in 1569 was the last flicker of their power, which Elizabeth crushed easily and without mercy.

The country squire

In their place were the gentry, a class of well-to-do knights and squires, some belonging to ancient families, but some who had recently acquired wealth and land, through trade, the law or good farming. Foreigners noticed that Englishmen, unlike the French and Italians, would leave the town when they had prospered, to set up house in the country and to take the lead in local affairs.

This class of squires, from which England drew its

leaders, adopted the sensible custom of putting their younger sons to trade or business instead of allowing them to lounge at home. Thus, while the eldest son learned to manage the family estates, his brothers became lawyers, parsons, merchant-adventurers, and the youngest served his time as a mercer's apprentice.

THE UNEMPLOYED

The country was prosperous and, beneath the gentry, there were classes of merchants, craftsmen, labourers and apprentices busily engaged in their occupations, but there were also men without work whose presence troubled the Queen's Council.

The population increases

By Tudor times, the population had recovered from the Black Death and was slowly increasing, so that each year there were more men than jobs and too little land for them to work. The "sturdy beggars" of the early Tudor reigns—the old soldiers, retainers and serving-men set adrift after the wars, who terrorised small towns and lonely travellers —were less of a problem now that the country was more orderly. But beggars and unemployed still wandered into London or moved on from place to place because no town would have them.

Some of the workless were countrymen who had lost their jobs through Enclosures, or had taken a sum for their strips of land and gone to the town and failed. Some had been unable to pay higher rent when the lease ran out, some were out of work because of a set-back in the cloth trade ; a few may have been bowyers, fletchers and armourers displaced by the new gun-making, and many were merely old or crippled, lazy, dishonest or feeble-minded.

Naturally, the rogues and vagabonds made for London, whose crowded streets offered better pick-

WORKING IN THE KITCHEN OF A BIG HOUSE

MANY POOR PEOPLE LIVED IN WRETCHED CONDITIONS

ings than any forest lair. At every corner, beggars showed their sores or held up a withered limb ; some pretended to be mad and covered themselves with blood and dirt to win pity. Cut-purses found work wherever crowds gathered ; cheats and card-sharpers waited for country lads at the inns, and " hookers " removed goods from upper windows, while honest citizens were asleep.

In times past, the monasteries had fed many of the poor, though some said they had merely encouraged idlers. The gilds, too, had done a great deal of good work, but it was now time for the government to take a hand by punishing the rogues and helping the honest poor. Private help of the poor never failed in England, and up and down the country we can still see the schools and almshouses founded by well-to-do citizens to help the needy and save their own souls. There was many a will like Sir Robert Hitcham's :

> " and likewise I do will that they do build one or two almshouses, consisting of Twelve persons . . . of the poorest and decrepit people which shall have 2 shillings to be paid weekly during their lives. And also 40 shillings a year for a gown and firing."

In London, some of the religious foundations were saved from the Reformation grabbers ; there were Saint Bartholomew's and Saint Thomas's Hospitals for the sick, Christ's Hospital for poor children, Bethlehem Hospital, known as " Bedlam ", for the lunatics, and Bridewell, a " house of correction " for idle vagrants. There was also the hospital that Sir John Hawkins gave for old sailors, and many similar charitable houses and schools.

Elizabeth's Poor Law of 1601 made it the duty of every parish to look after its poor. The Justices had to see that a rate was

USING AN ADZE TO SMOOTH A LOG

collected and that Overseers of the Poor bought "a stock of flax, hemp, wool, thread, iron and other stuff to set the poor to work" in the workhouse. The goods they made were to be sold at market rates to pay for their lodging and to teach their children a trade. The law was not always carried out wisely or generously, but it was a start that no other country had made.

A SOLDIER WITH AN ARQUEBUS. BY HIS SIDE HANGS A POWDER HORN AND IN HIS LEFT HAND IS A BURNING FUSE

THE FREE ENGLISHMAN

But if there was poverty, there was also general prosperity. The Reverend Harrison, who wrote a book about England, noticed that, whereas "in old time", farmers "were scarce able to live and pay their rent without selling of a cow or an horse", the Elizabethan farmer now had "a fair garnish of pewter on his cupboard, three or four feather beds, so many coverlets and carpets of tapestry, a silver salt, a bowl for wine and a dozen of spoons".

This prosperity had come from peace in the kingdom, from better farming, increased manufactures and new markets abroad. These were far more valuable than all the gold that Drake and the freebooters might bring home from the New World.

The true Elizabethan

Thus, after the Armada, the Englishman looked at the world with growing confidence, proud of what he had done, proud of being English and free from oppression. He hated professional soldiers and therefore liked the Tudors because they kept no standing army, and would allow the nobles none either. His old masters, the abbots and great lords, had gone, but he did not fear or hate the gentry, for he was free to speak out and to make his own way in the world. Unless he was an ardent Catholic or a Puritan, he felt there ought to be one religion in the land with the Queen at its head. He liked sermons and did not mind going to church to sing and pray in his own language. He certainly had no time for the Pope, a mere foreign bishop, and not much for the Puritan merchant who wanted to stop merry-making and bear-baiting.

Every parish kept armour, pikes, bows and one or two handguns (calivers and arquebuses) in some central place, usually the church, to equip three or four men, " as one archer, one gunner, one pike and a billman ", if that was the parish levy.

The Englishman did not think of military service as something hurtful to free men. He took up his arms to defend his own land with the same readiness as the merchant seamen and coastal sailors sallied out with Howard to join the Queen's ships against the enemy.

The spirit of the Elizabethan age

This eager spirit was the mark of the Elizabethan. No other reign, except Victoria's, when the population was six or seven times greater, produced so many men whose names still inspire us with a feeling that they were larger than life. Inquisitive, tireless and full of zest, they had the boundless energy that men and women find when enthusiasm is running high. This small society bore poets and writers like Sidney, Spenser, Raleigh, Gilbert and Francis Bacon, whose everyday lives were devoted to soldiering, politics and adventure. It was the hey-day of the all-rounder, when sea-captains wrote books, and poets experimented with farming and science, designed their own houses and went to the wars or the Indies. In under thirty years, the Elizabethans produced more poetry, drama, essays, music and philosophy than in two centuries before them.

LONGBOWMEN AND A PIKEMAN

HARDWICK HALL, DERBYSHIRE

CHAPTER 8

THE ELIZABETHANS AT HOME

HOUSES

It was an enthusiastic age for building, not churches, but new houses. Gone was the need for moats, narrow windows and an encircling wall.

New houses

The great houses going up in the country looked out on the world, not to repulse enemies but to welcome their guests from windows as high as the rooms themselves. England now had her own glass works and, though large sheets could not yet be made, small panes were held by lead strips to make bigger windows than anyone had known before. The old jibe about Bess of Hardwick's great house :

" Hardwick Hall,
More glass than wall,"

reminds us of the shocked surprise that greeted the first glass-and-concrete schools after the 1939–45 war.

The wealthy landowner occasionally altered his home but more often pulled down the old manor-house. Then he built anew, not in rambling fashion, but in the shape of an H or an E, with pinnacles, turrets and wings matching each other, or very nearly. From a variety of styles, using columns, porches, bay-windows, turrets and curious chimneys, he somehow built a house that was extraordinarily attractive and entirely English.

TUDOR CHIMNEYS

The materials nearest to hand were used—stone in the Midlands and West, bricks in East Anglia and, wherever oak was plentiful, timber, with plain or decorated plaster between the beams, to produce the lovely black and white houses, like Moreton Old Hall and many a yeoman's farmhouse.

In the great houses, like Audley End, Hardwick, Montacute and Longleat, the Hall was the biggest room, because of tradition and the need for a room fit for banquets and revels. Everyday family life went on in smaller dining-rooms and parlours. Kitchen, buttery and dairy were on the ground floor, no longer separate buildings, and a splendid staircase led upstairs to the library, the bed-chambers and the Long Gallery. Here was the best furniture, the finest panelling and one or two magnificent fireplaces. The great windows, all along one side and sometimes at the ends, allowed visitors to look across the deer park and down upon the clipped maze and the neat pattern of the garden.

THE LONG GALLERY OF AN ELIZABETHAN HOUSE

The Long Gallery was the centre and the glory of the great house, with its multitude of relatives, cousins, spinster aunts, guests, tutor, Italian dancing master, chaplain and secretary. Here they walked up and down, sewed, played backgammon and noisier games, learned their lessons, practised fencing, sang to the flutes and viols, and doubtless held hands and whispered love sonnets in the window seats.

Smaller country manors and the better town houses reflected the style of the wealthy, with " three or four bay-windows well-glased and three goodly chimneys." Some of the older people thought that the modern ideas were a sign that Englishmen were going soft . William Harrison acidly remarked :

> " Now we have manie chimneys, and yet our tenderlings complain of rheumes, catarhs and poses (colds). Then we had none but reredosses (iron firebacks) and our heads did never ake. For as the smoke in those days was supposed to be a sufficient hardening of the timber of the house, so it was reputed to keepe the good man and his familie from the quake (illness)."

Even if wood-smoke had been good for the health as well as the beams, everyone who could afford it was adding a chimney to one end of his house, now that a plentiful supply of bricks made it possible to do this without endangering the timber-framed house.

GARDENS

Elizabethan gardens were planned almost as carefully as the house itself. All was neatness, with straight walks and flower-beds bordered by tiny hedges of box to form an elaborate geometrical pattern known as a " knot ". Covered walks, clipped yews, bushes cut in weird shapes, fountains and lawns were all arranged with trim accuracy. Travellers

TUDOR FURNITURE

THE GARDEN WAS PLANNED AS CAREFULLY AS THE HOUSE

brought new plants from abroad, and the favourites then are still our favourite flowers today—roses, carnations, marigolds, stocks, wallflowers, pinks, larkspur, violets and lilacs. " Gillyflowers " seem to have been any sweet-scented flowers ; many were used in making jams, soap, and toilet water for the fingers after dinner.

The herb garden

The herb garden was of great importance to the housewife. She used herbs not only for cooking, for medicines and ointments, but also for hanging up in the rooms to sweeten the air : a Venetian visitor remarked, " Over the floors they strew weeds called rushes which grow on the water, and aloft at the window sills they put rosemary, sage and other herbs." " Other herbs " included balm, thyme, lavender and marjoram, but there must have been many others for a famous herbalist who had a " physic garden " in Holborn was said to have 1,000 different kinds, and old William Harrison had 300 varieties in his garden.

FURNITURE

For all their extravagance and love of display, the Tudors had little furniture in their great rooms.

The only really comfortable piece of furniture in the house was the huge four-poster bed, with its velvet and silk hangings to keep out the harmful night air. The custom of passing on the family bed from father to son was still observed, as can be seen in the will of the Duke of Norfolk, one of the greatest nobles in the kingdom :

> " to our sonne and heire, our great hanged bedde, with cloth of golde, whyte damask and black velvet, and our hangying (tapestry) of the story of Hercules made for our great chamber at Framlyngham."

As a good husband, the Duke left his wife all the other household goods :

> " To our wyfe Agnes all manner of plate, jewels . . . all our household stuff, beddings, hangings, fustians, blankets, pelows (pillows), cushions, hanged beds of gold and silk . . . all our naprie (linen), all our chapel stuff, with all manner of kitchen stuff . . . with all our horses, harness, long-bowes, cross bowes, all our ringes, jewels of gold . . . and all our other goods and chattels."

Thus, the only pieces of furniture mentioned by name are the beds, the rest are " goods and chattels." These would include the trestle tables in the Hall, the new " joined " table with its bulbous legs, stools and only two or three chairs, whose hard seats were improved with cushions. In 1556, Sir John Gage left as many as 43 cushions, as well as some chests, which were still used for storing household goods.

In the parlour, there was probably a cupboard with shelves for plates, and these shelves might be enclosed by doors to make a livery or dole cupboard

TUDOR FURNITURE

containing " livery ", bread, butter, cheese, candles, etc. to be " doled " out to the servants. The court-cupboard held wine, linen and dry goods for the mistress' table.

The bed-chamber

In the bed-chamber, there was often a low truckle bed for a child or a servant to sleep on, and this could be pushed under the big bed in daytime. A " press " (wardrobe) held clothes, and, on a chest, stood a basin and ewer, with pots of complexion paint and perfumes. Only a wealthy home would have a real looking-glass, for most ladies had to make do with a mirror of polished metal.

Tapestries, as well as panelling, covered the walls, though portraits were becoming fashionable. Eastern rugs and Turkey carpets were too valuable to be put on the floor, except for the Queen's feet ; normally, the flagstones were strewn with rushes and straw which were not renewed until they stank.

SANITATION AND CLEANLINESS

The little tablets, made from flowers and spices, that were burned to give off a pleasant odour, the flowering sprigs and scented herbs placed about the house helped to disguise the strong smells inside and out. Rubbish and slops were thrown out of the doors and windows and left where they fell. In towns, the stink from rotting garbage must have been appalling, but no one minded unless the way was blocked.

Every now and then, dust-carts came round to clear the streets of dung and rubbish, which was dumped just outside the walls or into the river.

Piped water was a rarity, for the country relied on its wells, and the towns upon the pump, stone cisterns, water-sellers and open conduits—narrow gullies that brought water from the river or town ditch.

Sanitation

The word " lavatory " really means a washing-place, and the room sometimes called " the toilet " nowadays was known to Elizabethans as a " house of easement " or " the privy ", i.e., " private place ". In medieval castles the privies, built into the thickness of the walls, were made to empty into the moat and, in monasteries, the " rere-dorter " was built over the river, but in Tudor times, the earth-closet was in the cellar or in a corner of the yard, which must have been much less satisfactory. In 1594, Sir John Harrington actually invented a water-closet, not unlike those of today, but, although the Queen had one installed in Richmond Place, people thought this was far too much of a fanciful notion for private houses.

The housewife made soap at home but too much washing was thought bad for the health. Even the laundering of household linen was held at monthly or longer intervals, when the woman servants got up at dawn for a mammoth washday. When we think of the heavy, embroidered clothes, padded, jewelled and kept for generations, it is clear that scents and perfumes were needed to disguise the smell of stale sweat and unwashed bodies.

Tooth-brushes were not yet in use, but tooth-soap could be made from the burned heads of mice, though an alternative, made with honey, vinegar and white wine boiled together, must have been more pleasant ! Everyone used toothpicks, and dental decay seems to have been less common than today, though a foreigner noticed that English people's teeth, even the old Queen's, were black through eating too many sweets.

TUDOR BONNETS

ELIZABETHAN COTTAGES IN NORTHAMPTONSHIRE

CLOTHES

When, in the reign of Elizabeth's father, the Earl of Surrey was executed, his gorgeous apparel was distributed, as was customary, to certain gentlemen. The list included:

The Earl of Surrey's apparel

> "a robe of purple velvet, four black velvet caps set with pearl and goldsmiths' work, a hat of crimson satin and velvet with a white feather, a scarf of crimson and gold, a robe with hood and crimson velvet, a gown with cloth of gold, furred and faced with sables, one of taffeta, several of satin, one with gold buttons enamelled black and white, a shirt wrought with black silk and a pair of hose, black velvet, with threads of Venice gold."

Doublets, padded and shaped with whalebone, were heavily embroidered, and cut, or "slashed", to show the gay linings. Giant sleeves ended in lace cuffs, and short cloaks, lined with satin or fur, were more

CLOSE-FITTING CAPS WERE OFTEN WORN

for show than protection. " Hose " did not mean stockings, but breeches, which, according to fashion, came almost to the knee, or were very short and so padded out with horse-hair, that the wearer could not sit on an ordinary chair.

Women's clothes were equally gorgeous and probably even more uncomfortable. Ladies wore leather corsets, with a laced-on piece, known as a " stomacher ", and their stiffened bodices flared out into huge skirts, worn, in the latter part of the reign, over a hoop fitted round the hips. This skirt was the farthingale, which roused the mirth of some and the contempt of the Puritans, in their sober dress and white collars.

Men and women of quality wore collars which began as frills, known as " piccadils " (hence, Piccadilly). These became larger, and were pleated and wired until they developed into ruffs, starched by a secret process from Holland, and into immense fan-shaped collars standing up behind the head. Ordinary citizens did not dare to copy the fashions of Court, even if they could have afforded them, though the wives of rich merchants did their discreet best. Apprentices, in particular, were forbidden to wear ruffs or silk doublets.

The Queen the centre of fashion

The Queen was the centre of fashion, possessing, it is said, a thousand dresses, many of them covered with small jewels and pearls. Fans and gloves were carried, and stockings, laced at the ankle to fit snugly, were made of wool or linen, though the Queen had several pairs of yellow silk.

Men wore shirts and " drawers " under their finery, while ladies' underclothes consisted of chemise, or " shift ", and petticoats, but night-dresses, known as " night rails " were quite the latest thing. Most people went to bed in a shift or nothing at all. A garment called a " night-dress " was what we should call a dressing-gown, and was made of heavy material trimmed with fur.

Fur had kept its popularity from the Middle Ages, partly as a sign of wealth and partly for warmth, since, as an Italian remarked :

> " In England it is always windy, and however warm the weather, the natives wear furs."

He also noticed that ladies wore velvet caps, muslin head-dresses, kerchiefs or white caps, but never showed their hair outdoors. At Court, red hair and wigs were worn by the ladies in honour of the Queen, who is said to have started the fashion to cover up her own falling locks.

THE FARTHINGALE WAS A HUGE SKIRT WORN OVER A HOOP WHICH FITTED ROUND THE HIPS

FOOD

The Englishman's food

The English had long been famous for their appetites, and foreigners, especially from warmer countries, were astonished at the vast quantities of meat they ate. Even the poor man fed far better than peasants abroad, enjoying his bacon and rabbit when he could not get beef, and only falling back on vegetable broth when times were bad.

The main meals were dinner, taken at about 11 o'clock (remember that the working day started very early), with the servants eating at noon, and supper at five or six. Although breakfast was not considered a meal, a snack of meat, bread and ale was usual, especially for the youngsters, and the Queen had chickens, rabbits, mutton, veal and beef, with ale and wine, served early in the morning.

At dinner, as much food as possible was put on the table at once, to show the master's wealth. Helpings of mutton, beef, pork and venison, not in slices but in lumps or " gobbets ", were followed by fish, game and poultry, and then by elaborate sweets and puddings, often shaped like animals or castles.

MEN WORE COLLARS KNOWN AS " PICCADILS "

THE INGLE NOOK OF AN ELIZABETHAN FARM HOUSE

CHAPTER 9

AT WORK AND PLAY

THE HOUSEWIFE

Marriage at an early age

OF all the contrasts between the Elizabethans and ourselves, the greatest is in the life of the housewife. To begin with, she was married at an age when our girls are still in school, and if she belonged to a family of any standing, her husband was chosen for her by her parents. Girls " came out " into society when they were about twelve, and were often married at thirteen or fourteen, and nearly always before they were eighteen. The famous Bess of Hardwick, Countess of Shrewsbury, was a widow at fourteen, with a fortune !

Sometimes children only three or four years old were married in church, and then returned to their

WOMEN OFTEN RODE BEHIND THEIR HUSBANDS

parents to be brought up until old enough to set up house. These child-marriages, which were really family alliances to secure land and property, could be set aside by the Bishop. Some girls were bold enough to defy their parents but most obeyed meekly, though in humble homes, where there was little money, a girl could doubtless marry for love.

Once married, the gentleman's wife took charge of a large household, with its small army of servants and female relatives. Up at dawn, she would go first to her prayers, and then to set the women to work in the kitchen. Next, she must plan, not merely the meals for that day or week, but for months ahead, laying in stores for the winter, when roads were impassable and fresh food hard to come by.

The work of the housewife

Meat and fish had to be salted, hams cured, jams, pickles and vegetables preserved. The girls must be kept at the spinning wheel, and the sewing women busy with their needles, for all linen and clothes, except the grandest, were made at home.

Innumerable jobs, which we avoid merely by walking into a shop, had to be done laboriously. Bread, for instance, was baked in vast quantities, fat had to be saved for candles and soap, feathers had to be cleaned for pillows and beds, dyes prepared for home-spun cloth, clean rushes gathered for the floors, and honey brought in from the hives.

Above all, the housewife must understand the making of medicines, " salves " and ointments, for which herbs and wild plants were gathered. Illness and accidents were common in a big household, so there was many a fever to be treated or injured limb to dress. Much of the housewife's time would be spent in the nursery, for she had a baby every year while she was young, though most of them died before they left the cradle. She must see that the little ones learned to read and behave themselves at

PEWTER TANKARDS AND UTENSILS

family prayers, when, every day in the parlour, her husband read from the Bible to the whole household, including the servants.

CHILDREN AND SCHOOLS

A CHILD'S HORN-BOOK

Children were lucky to survive infancy, for everything, except the natural toughness of Elizabethans, was against them from the start. At birth, mothers were attended by a midwife who knew more about charms against witchcraft than about hygiene. In babyhood, the child was wrapped in a cocoon of swaddling clothes, petted and fussed in his wooden cradle by the fire, and almost smothered with blankets and pillows.

If he survived this treatment, the germs and unsuitable food—ale, mutton bones and a manchet (a small loaf) for breakfast—the child had to grow up quickly when he was out of the cradle. He started lessons very young, ate grown-up food and dressed in clothes that were almost exactly like an adult's. Children called their parents " Sir " and " Madam ", removed their hats when speaking, and even knelt down to make a request. The slightest disobedience or fault was punished by a whipping, which was believed to be the best treatment for children and servants.

Little children were taught to read at home from a horn-book, a bat-shaped piece of wood, on which was pasted a sheet with the letters of the alphabet, beginning with a " Christ cross ". There were also the vowels, some useful syllables and the Lord's Prayer, all covered by a piece of thin horn, so the " book " lasted for years, and was handed on from child to child in the family.

AN ELIZABETHAN SCHOOL DESK

Latin, French and Greek at the age of five

Regular lessons began at an alarmingly early age. We hear of tiny mites of three and four years learning Latin and French, and of a boy who, at five, " had a strong passion for Greek ", and knew more Latin than most boys of ten or twelve. The father of a certain Thomas Slingsby was worried that his son, aged five, liked play better than lessons—" I find him duller *this year* than last . . . but I think it to be his too much minding Play which takes his mind from his books."

MOST CHILDREN HAD SOME SCHOOLING

When they were old enough, boys, and sometimes girls too, went on to the local Grammar School, and some to the boarding schools, such as Eton, Winchester and Westminster, where the Master of the School was paid £24 a year for a boy's food, besides " something " for schooling. Then, as now, a boarding education was expensive, but there were forty King's Scholars who had free places and a new gown every year.

Harrison tells us that there were not many towns in England without a Grammar School to take bright boys from poor homes. At the Merchant Taylors School, there were 100 free places, and at St. Paul's School, " one hundred and fifty-three poor men's children ", though these were much larger schools than those in country towns, where men like William Harpur, Mayor of Bedford, founded a free school, as did Sir Roger Manwood at Sandwich, Sir John Gresham at Holt, Sir Andrew Judd at Tonbridge, and many others.

A master and an usher, teaching all subjects in one large room, seem to have been the entire staff of the small grammar school. At Ipswich, the room was the old refectory of the monastery, a huge place, 120 feet long, though the original schoolroom

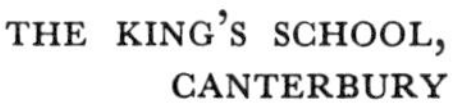

THE KING'S SCHOOL, CANTERBURY

A CHOIRBOY

had fallen down. Here, Queen Elizabeth's charter awarded the handsome salary of £24. 6s. 8d. to the master, and £14. 6s. 8d. to the usher, to be paid out of certain farm rents. The boys, about 30 in number, were generally the sons of burgesses in the town, with a few " gentlemen's sons " ; they had to bring their own books, paper, pens and ink, for which poor scholars received a sum every year, while the rest paid according to their fathers' rank. Hours were longer and holidays shorter than today. At Ashby-de-la-Zouch, the master wrote, " the school-time should begin at six ", and there was to be Latin until nine, then a break of quarter of an hour, and school again until eleven. After dinner, lessons went on until half past five ending with a psalm and prayers.

The schoolboy's day

The principal subjects were Latin, which the boys often had to speak all day long, some Greek and Hebrew, and a little arithmetic. There seems to have been no English, while French and Italian were left to the tutors at home. There were also subjects called logic and rhetoric (oral debate), but History and Geography (called Cosmography when it included astronomy) were not taken until at University.

Schooling for all except the poor

All, except the children of unskilled labourers, had some schooling, for those who could not manage a place at the grammar school, would attend for a year or two the Dame School, where a woman or sometimes a master, taught them to read and write. As a countryman said :

> " this is all we go to school for ; to read Common Prayers at church and set down common prices at Market ; write a letter and make a Bond (a legal agreement), set down the day of our Births, our Marriage day and make our Wills when we are sicke."

ELIZABETHAN COINS

WORK

Besides the industries in cottage, woodlands and mines, there were so many new opportunities that the Elizabethan age was a small industrial revolution in itself. There were the glass and brick-making trades, the salt industry, soap and dye-making, iron-smelting, button and pin manufacture, guns and cannons for sale abroad, as well as at home. Sugar-refining, brought to London from Antwerp, was a new business, and so was the first paper-mill at Dartford, which produced white paper for the thriving printers and book-binders.

The cloth trade, still booming, was given fresh life by the Protestant refugees from abroad. Flemings and Huguenots brought special weaving skills and secrets with them, though some places did not welcome the strangers. Norwich showed more sense and, by 1572, had 4,000 foreign weavers in the city ; there were over 500 at Colchester, more than 400 in Sandwich, some at Maidstone and Canterbury and many at Ipswich. They introduced linen and sailcloth manufacture, silk weaving, needlemaking and new pottery methods. It is in the cloth trade that we find the start of factories, for a poem of the time tells of a work-place which employed 200 weavers, with 200 spinning women, 100 more to card wool that had been picked and sorted by little children, and there were dyers and fullers to finish the cloth.

With this great increase in trade went some of the ups and downs of business—masters could go bankrupt, trade sometimes was slack, and standards of work might fall without proper supervision. In 1563, the *Statute of Artificers* (the word means " workmen ") laid down many rules, of which the best known is the binding of apprentices for seven years. No man could set up in a Craft without this long training, but there

AN EARLY COAL MINE

CHILDREN WERE DRESSED LIKE THEIR ELDERS

were many workers besides the fully trained " craftsmen ", and they, too, were looked after.

The working day was extremely long. A law of Henry VIII's reign laid down that craftsmen and labourers were to be at work in summer *before five o'clock in the morning*, and to continue until seven or eight at night, with only half an hour for breakfast and up to one and a half hours for dinner. In winter, they merely had to start at dawn, and " depart not till night " !

GAMES, SPORTS AND PASTIMES

Some of the games we play today were already old in Elizabeth's reign. There were chasing games, like hide-and-seek, blindman's buff, and prisoner's base ; there were ball games, such as stool-ball, tennis, bowls, handball and football, as well as skittles, or *kayles*, where a short stick was aimed at the pins. " Ten-pins " must have been similar, and there was *tip-cat*, played like a simple form of cricket, except that for ball there was a stick, or " cat ", about six inches long which the bowler tried to pitch into a circle, twelve paces away.

Football, with no marked pitch and no rules, was a glorious free-for-all, with a ball to kick at occasionally ! Quieter games were *fives*, played against the church wall, and *bandy-ball*, a fore-runner of golf or hockey.

Popular amusements

Popular games indoors were chess, draughts, quoits, backgammon (played with dice and " men ", on a board), *slide-thrift* or shove ha'penny, and, of course, dice and cards, which the Puritans frowned upon.

Outdoors, running races, jumping contests, wrestling and *quarter-staff* matches were held on festival days, but *archery* still held pride

BOYS PRACTISING ARCHERY

of place for skill, and there were few who would have agreed that the days of the bow as a weapon were almost over.

Everyone, from the Queen down, had a passion for *hunting*, and it was typical of the Tudor age that poor men were not savagely punished for joining in, as in former times and in days to come. The rich hunted deer across their parks, while farmers and villagers chased hare and rabbit across country with packs of small dogs. The fox was regarded as vermin to be killed on sight and his head nailed to the church door when the church-warden had paid the fee for the kill. *Hawking* had not yet died out, and would not do so until firearms became more accurate.

Bear-baiting was as popular as ever, and the Queen herself enjoyed the shows put on for her entertainment. In villages and towns, the bear was chained to a post on the green, but special courts were built, as at the Paris Gardens, in Southwark, across the Thames, and at Kenilworth, with seats for spectators. The captive bear was attacked by five or six fierce mastiffs, called *bandogs*, which were killed or maimed in the battle. Oddly enough, the bear was regarded with affection, and carefully nursed back to health if wounded. There are stories of more than one village selling its church Bible to buy a bear !

FESTIVALS

Much more pleasant, but still attacked by the Puritans, were the revels that took place on festival days, such as May Day, Midsummer Eve, Christmas, Plough Monday and Shrove Tuesday.

On May Day, the lads and lasses went out early to the woods to gather flowers and green branches, the girls washing their faces

APPRENTICES OFTEN PLAYED FOOTBALL IN THE STREETS

PLAYING THE PIPE AND DRUM

in the dew to bring beauty. Then, accompanied by all the villagers, a great pole, decorated with flowers and boughs, was hauled by oxen, also decked with posies, to the Green, where it was set up on its stone base and "bound round with strings from top to bottom, painted in variable colours . . . with handkerchiefs and streaming flags on top". Then the people "set up summer halls, bowers and arbours about it and then fall to banqueting and feasting, to leaping and dancing about it".

DANCING AND MUSIC

Formal dances at Court

Dances, like the morris-dance and the horn-dance by men wearing antlers, took place outdoors, and besides the expert performance of the dancing teams, there was a great deal of lively jigging and capering to pipe and drum. Court dances, however, were formal and complicated, and could only be learned from a dancing master, who taught the stately *pavane* and the spirited *galliard*, with its quick leaps and twirls.

A foreign visitor noted in 1598, "the English excel in dancing and music, for they are lively and active", and for 150 years England was the most renowned nation in Europe for its music and singing. The new church services of the Reformation required a new music, and several composers, of whom William Byrd was the greatest, wrote some magnificent music for psalms and anthems. The singing in church was wonderfully good, and many of the cathedrals installed organs.

Ordinary citizens, as well as the gentry and courtiers, delighted in singing unaccompanied rounds, catches and madrigals, and it was thought proper for an educated person to be able to read music at sight and play at least one instrument. The merchant's parlour and the Long Gallery had their viols, lutes, harpsichord, recorders and shawms with which to entertain their guests and themselves. Certain towns

MORRIS DANCING ON THE GREEN

even employed minstrels to play at the festivals, and "waits" to go about the streets making music for the pleasure of the burgesses.

A LUTE AND A RECORDER

LONDON

At this time, London was more important even than today. No other city in the country had a tenth of its population or wealth, and none could rival its trade, for its customs duties brought in twenty times as much as at Bristol, the second port of the kingdom.

But the modern sprawl of London had hardly begun, and it was still a recognisable city, with its walls and gates—Ludgate, Newgate, Aldersgate, Moorgate, Cripplegate, Aldgate and Bishopsgate—in good repair. Certainly, the houses were spreading beyond the walls, but there were open fields nearby and, within the city, many a garden and orchard.

On the east, stood the dreaded Tower of London with its apartments for State prisoners, and a menagerie of wild animals. To the west, lay Westminster, a maze of courts and chambers known as the Palace, from which the Queen ruled. Behind the walls of the city, the Mayor and his aldermen were well-nigh supreme, for the noblemen had moved out to big houses along the Strand leading to Westminster.

NEWGATE

Nowhere else in England was there a city with the independence of London. The Government passed its wishes to the Lord Mayor, who carried them out through the leading personages of the City Companies, such as the Drapers, Merchant Taylors, Grocers, Goldsmiths, Mercers, Stationers, Pewterers, Fishmongers and Skinners. These Companies, which had developed from the gilds, were enormously rich and powerful, and it was they who regulated life in the city, controlled its trade and protected its orphans, aged and sick.

A WATER-CARRIER

The City Companies

The sober aldermen and prosperous citizens were stoutly Protestant, even Puritan, and though they had lawless characters in plenty to keep in order they did their best to uphold the Watch and put down the rowdies. Their strict rule and a regulation of 1588 ordering every householder to provide a light at his door, caused many a murderer and thief to take himself across the river where, at Bankside and Southwark, were to be found the slums, low taverns, the Bear Garden and the new theatres.

As they came up the Thames, foreigners and returning Englishmen saw a beautiful city, the greatest in Europe, its buildings and spires shining in the clear air with the great spire of Old St. Paul's, 150 ft. higher than the present dome, towering over all, until destroyed by lightning in 1561. No capital could

LONDON BRIDGE, WITH ITS TALL HOUSES AND SHOPS, WAS ONE OF THE WONDERS OF THE WORLD

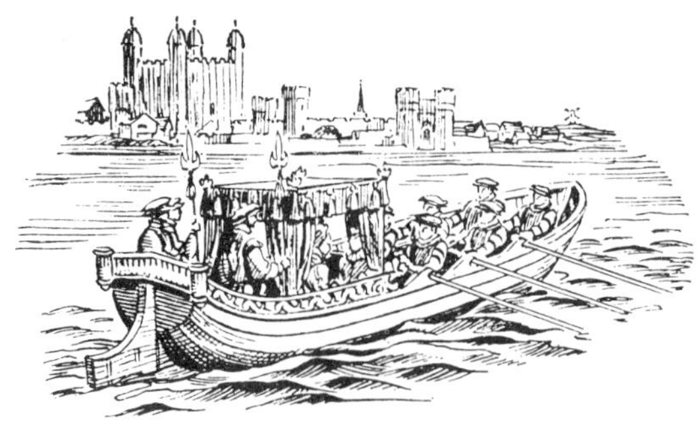

THE ROYAL BARGE PASSES THE TOWER OF LONDON ON ITS WAY TO GREENWICH

equal the splendid waterfront, with its flights of steps, its wharves and cranes unloading the merchant ships, while skiffs and wherries darted about with goods and passengers. The Thames was the chief highway, on which the royal barge might be seen taking the Queen down to her favourite palace at Greenwich.

London Bridge was one of the wonders of the world, with its tall houses and shops, and the ghastly row of heads upon the gateway at the southern end. The river rushed so furiously under the narrow arches that " shooting the bridge " was a well-known thrill, though nervous passengers went ashore and re-embarked on the other side.

THE CITY OF LONDON WAS OVERCROWDED ; ITS NARROW LANES WERE MUDDY AND ILL-PAVED

A STREET QUACK

But if it was beautiful from the river, the city was overcrowded. The wooden houses of the poor, harbouring rats, and the narrow lanes, stinking with garbage, were breeding-places for disease. The plague came every year, and was worst in hot summers, which caused severe outbreaks in 1563, in 1592-4 and in 1603. Normal life was interrupted, for the wealthy departed to the country, and shops and places of amusement were closed, until cooler weather lessened the disease. The poor suffered most, for they lived in the worst conditions, and one of the problems of the time was to find burial space for the dead.

THEATRES

Professional actors

From the medieval players and the choir-boys of the Chapel Royal, a body of professional actors arose who had to be under the protection of some great man—the Earl of Leicester or the Lord Admiral—lest they be taken up as rogues and vagabonds. They toured the country, giving performances in the yards of inns and at the houses of noblemen, for it was the gentry and the humble citizens who loved the play, rather than the respectable merchant-class.

SHAKESPEARE'S FIRST THEATRE WAS BUILT OUTSIDE THE CITY OF LONDON, AT SHOREDITCH

When the companies came to London and were in trouble with the Lord Mayor for causing crowds to collect (thus spreading disease or disorder), it was the Privy Council that defended the actors. It pointed out that Her Majesty " Sometimes took delight in these pastimes ", and it was desirable for the players to have practice to be " in readiness . . . for her Highness' solace next Christmas ".

Theatres built outside the City

But the City of London made life so irksome for actors that the earliest theatres, the " Theatre " and the " Curtain ", were built outside at Shoreditch. New theatres were built across the river, where the " Rose " and the " Swan " were followed by the " Globe ", erected in 1599 by Burbage and a group of shareholders who included a certain William Shakespeare. These early theatres were built round an open " pit ", into which the stage jutted, to give a good view to the " quality " in the balconies.

Between 1580 and 1590, a group of dramatists, led by Marlowe, Peel, Nash and Greene, were writing plays for the companies of actors, plays full of action and poetry, of old ideas and clumsy violence. Then

THE STAGE JUTTED OUT INTO THE PIT OF THE THEATRE

William Shakespeare

there arrived in London, a man from Stratford-on-Avon, a fair actor himself, who adapted historical stories, Italian tales, old plots and popular characters, and turned them into the greatest plays ever written in any language.

Shakespeare was a miracle, a genius who occurred at exactly the right moment of history—or was it the age that made him? Poetry was in the air, it was the time-honoured language of minstrel and entertainer, given new form and beauty by such poets as Spenser, Sidney and Marlowe. Great events and great men were on everyone's lips, and there was a spirit of confidence, with all the excitement of new ideas, new discoveries, travellers, foreigners and wealth flooding into the teeming capital. A playwright with a genius for expressing character—kings, nagging wives, fat rascals, comical workmen and young lovers—could flourish in this golden age and write the plays that are England's greatest triumph.

THE "ROSE" AND THE "GLOBE" THEATRES, WHERE SHAKESPEARE'S PLAYS WERE PERFORMED

PART TWO

THE STUARTS

CHAPTER 10

KING JAMES I

Royal progress from Scotland

THE son of Mary Queen of Scots and Lord Darnley was thirty-six when he received the longed-for news that his relation Elizabeth was dead. Almost at once he set out on the leisurely journey to London. On the way, James accepted with great good humour the hospitality, the days of hunting, the bell-ringing and welcoming stares of his new subjects. They received him with relief, for he was a Protestant of Tudor descent, and there was no prospect of foreign interference with the Succession. People noticed, however, that the King had neither the appearance nor the royal bearing of his cousin.

James shambled on spindly legs, and was usually to be seen leaning on the shoulder of a Court favourite. He looked better on horseback, for he rode well and possessed the royal passion for hunting. Nowadays, it would be said that the King suffered from a " speech defect ", since he spoke " with a plum in his mouth ", and had a curious habit of lolling out his tongue as though it were too big for his mouth. Men declared that he never washed, but merely rubbed his fingers with a napkin, and his table manners were shocking, even in a coarse age. As for dress, James never seemed to mind how shabby his clothes were, so long as his doublets were sufficiently padded to resist a dagger-thrust.

KING JAMES I

A GENTLEMAN WITH HIS FALCON

The King's character was as curious as his appearance. Already famous for his learning and for his witty sayings, he became an expert on many subjects, including witchcraft and religion. But he was so conceited about his own cleverness that he imagined all other men were fools. However, he was good-humoured, and he genuinely hated cruelty and war. Affectionate and generous to his friends, he had absolutely no judgement of men, no tact and no understanding of the people he had come to rule.

THE KING WHO DISAPPOINTED EVERYONE

Both the Puritans and the Catholics hoped that they would have an easier time under James than in Elizabeth's latter years.

During the journey from Scotland, a body of Puritan clergymen presented a petition, asking if they could leave out some of the ceremonies in the Church services, such as the giving of a ring in marriage, baptising an infant with the sign of the Cross, and bowing at the name of Jesus.

James angers the Puritans

James called these Puritan clergymen to discuss the matter with him at the *Hampton Court Conference*. Unfortunately, he looked on this as an opportunity to show off his own cleverness in religious debate. He made the mistake of thinking that English Puritans were no different from the Scottish Presbyterian ministers who had thundered away about the wickedness of Kings, when he was a boy. Suddenly losing his temper, he bellowed that he would make the Puritans conform, or " harry them out of the land ".

It was a disastrous mistake. A little commonsense and tact would have kept the Puritans in the Church ; instead, they were driven into opposition, and some 300 clergymen were expelled from the Church of England. Supported by their faithful

JAMES SHAMBLED ALONG ON HIS SPINDLY LEGS, OFTEN LEANING ON THE SHOULDER OF A FAVOURITE

A PRIEST GOES INTO THE " PRIEST-HOLE " IN THE WALL

congregations and utterly devoted to their beliefs, the " silenced brethren " grew in strength and influence, holding illegal meetings and services for their fellow " non-conformists ".

THE GUNPOWDER PLOT

The Catholics also had reason to hope for better days. The King's mother had died in their faith, and James had promised that they should not be molested.

Thus, it was believed that fines for staying away from church would be abolished and that Catholics would be free to worship openly. It would no longer be necessary to hold secret services at night in attics and cellars, while the priest hid all day in the tiny " priest-hole " behind the fireplace.

Any suggestion of gentleness towards the Catholic religion so alarmed the country that James took fright. He allowed Robert Cecil to banish priests and to reimpose harsh fines. The Catholics were bitterly disappointed, and a few desperate hot-heads began to plan revenge.

A small group of zealots, led by *Robert Catesby*, hatched a plot to destroy the King, Lords and Commons as they assembled for the opening of Parliament. Having wiped out the country's leaders, they hoped that an armed uprising and foreign invasion would bring about a Catholic triumph.

The conspirators began to dig a tunnel from the cellar of a building next to the Parliament House. Their expert on explosives and tunnelling was Guy Fawkes, a Yorkshire Catholic who had been serving in the Spanish armies of Flanders. A huge foundation wall baffled the tunnellers, until Fawkes discovered an easier solution. Strolling round to investigate a nearby rumbling noise, he discovered that

GUY FAWKES AND THE PLOTTERS

a lumber-room, running right underneath the House of Lords, was used as a store for coal and timber.

This room was hired, and Fawkes managed to place in it thirty-six barrels of gunpowder which he covered up with several loads of firewood. Meanwhile, the plotters dispersed to assemble arms and horses. Among those let into the secret was a man who wished to save a kinsman. Lord Monteagle received a letter warning him to stay away from Parliament :

The plot revealed

> " retire yourself into country, where you may expect the event in safety, for though there be no appearance of any stir, yet I say they shall receive a terrible blow this Parliament and they shall not see who hurts them."

When this letter was passed to the Government, the game was up, and Catesby and his friends hurried away from London.

Guy Fawkes, however, stuck to his post, hoping that coolness and daring would succeed. On the 4th of November 1605, a member of the Privy Council looked into the lumber-room and asked who owned the firewood : Fawkes answered cheerfully and still did not try to escape. At 11 o'clock that night, while he was taking the air outside, a party of soldiers went in to examine the faggots, and, a few moments later, Fawkes was knocked down and carried away to the Tower. He held out against torture until he learned that his fellow plotters had died at bay in a Staffordshire country house. Then, so maimed that he could not walk to the scaffold, he went bravely to his death.

The *Gunpowder Plot,* concocted by only a handful of desperadoes, ruined the Catholic cause in England. From now on, men regarded Catholics with the horror and detestation reserved for traitors who would kill the King to bring in a foreigner.

WHEN THE PLOT WAS DISCOVERED, CATESBY AND HIS FRIENDS HURRIED AWAY FROM LONDON

DIVINE RIGHT

James's attitude to Kingship

Having mortally offended the Puritans and reawakened hatred for the Catholics, James now proceeded to upset Parliament.

Elizabeth had often been out of patience with her " froward " parliaments, but she had realised their growing spirit of self-importance, and had never insulted them. James, believing himself as wise as Solomon, had worked out a theory about kingship which was certain to offend the squires and lawyers who were set upon having a larger say in the government of their country.

It has to be remembered that James had had a stormy upbringing. His father was murdered and his mother, thrust out by her own subjects, was later executed in England. As a child, James had been lectured by tutors and nagged by ministers. He was told over and over again that Kings were given their position by the people. He knew that William the Silent was assassinated and that his relative Elizabeth was constantly in danger of the same fate.

When he grew up, James wrote a book called *The True Law of Free Monarchies*, in which he stated that kings were appointed by God, and they ruled by *Divine Right*. A king was free to do as he pleased, and his subjects must merely obey. He wrote :

" Kings are justly called gods . . . they make and unmake their subjects . . . they have the power of raising up and casting down . . . of life and death . . . to make of their subjects like men at chess."

AS A CHILD, JAMES HAD BEEN LECTURED BY TUTORS AND NAGGED BY MINISTERS

TOBACCO WAS TAXED AS WELL AS CURRANTS AND OTHBR GOODS

This might have been said by Henry VIII, but in 1604, it was no way to talk to freeborn Englishmen. The gentry, prosperous and self-confident, did not feel themselves bound to James with the love and loyalty they had felt for the Great Queen. They were certainly not to be treated as chess-men.

PARLIAMENT

There was only one check on a king with these views. It was Parliament's ancient right to vote him the usual Customs Duties, which, with his private income, enabled him to run the country.

When Parliament therefore persisted in talking about its "ancient and undoubted right . . . to debate freely all matters," including the 300 "silenced" Puritan brethren, James decided to manage without Parliament. From 1611 to 1621, he somehow did so.

Rule without Parliament

The Court was corrupt and extravagant. James had little idea how to manage money and believed that England was inexhaustibly wealthy. Mean in some ways, he lavished gifts on his favourites, and spent more in peace than Elizabeth had done in her wars. He borrowed heavily in the City of London, tried to raise "benevolences", or forced loans, invented the title of baronet which rich men could buy or be fined for refusing, granted Monopolies and put taxes, called Impositions, on such goods as currants and tobacco. These money-raising devices made the King unpopular, without bringing in sufficient to make the Crown really independent of Parliament.

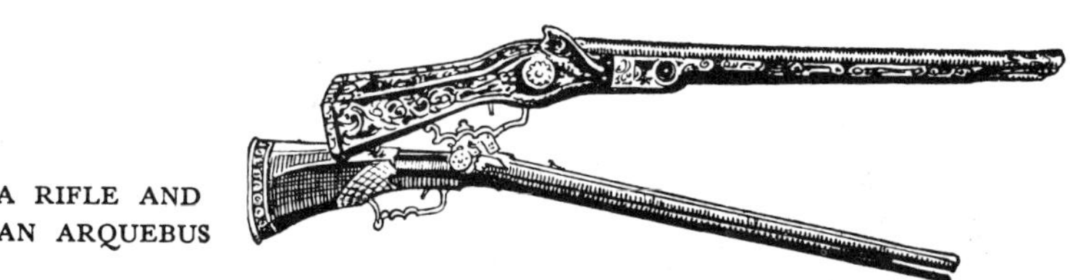
A RIFLE AND AN ARQUEBUS

FOREIGN AFFAIRS

The King, who hated violence, put an end to the Spanish war soon after his accession. Raleigh, one of the " men of war ", was kept for years in the Tower, and eventually executed for attacking the Spaniards on his ill-fated trip to Guiana. Believing that he could make peace between the Catholic and Protestant powers abroad, James arranged for his beautiful daughter, Elizabeth, to marry a Protestant prince, or Elector, of a part of Germany called the Palatine, and he planned to marry his son to a Catholic princess of Spain.

James tries to pacify Catholics and Protestants abroad

Elizabeth's husband, Frederick, was invited to become King of Bohemia, where the throne was vacant. The Emperor refused to allow such presumption, and Catholic armies from Austria, and Spanish troops from the Netherlands, drove out the Elector and his English queen. Thus began, in 1618, the bloodthirsty struggle in Germany, known as *The Thirty Years' War*.

James naturally wanted to help his daughter, who was now a fugitive without a kingdom, but his foolish policy had led him into a tangle. To promote the marriage of his son to the Infanta, he had curried favour with Spain, whose Ambassador became the most influential man in London. But Spanish troops were occupying the Palatine, and the King of Spain saw no reason to withdraw them, marriage or no marriage.

When Parliament was summoned, it was enthusiastic for a war to rescue the Protestant cause, but it was soon told that foreign policy was none of its business. In fact, England had no fleet or army worth talking about, and no knowledge of how to fight a war on the Continent.

GONDOMAR, THE SPANISH AMBASSADOR

THE SPANISH MATCH

Meanwhile, the King's plan for the Spanish Match horrified the country. Englishmen were in no mood to forgive their old enemy and to see a Catholic queen bringing up Catholic heirs to the throne.

James, fascinated by his favourite George Villiers, Duke of Buckingham and by Gondomar, the Spanish ambassador, hesitated, and then allowed a most foolish escapade to take place.

Prince Charles and Buckingham left the country secretly, crossed France in disguise, and appeared in Madrid to woo the princess. The Spaniards were astonished and suspicious, the prince was young and silly, and Buckingham behaved with insolence to his proud hosts.

GEORGE VILLIERS, DUKE OF BUCKINGHAM

The romantic trip was a ridiculous failure. The Spaniards said they would rather put the Infanta " headlong into a well " than into such hands, and the two young men came home without the lady. London greeted them with such relief and joy that Buckingham came to the conclusion that he must arrange a war instead of a marriage.

The foolish old King, disappointed in all his hopes, died next year. In his reign of twenty-two years, he had made England the laughing-stock of Europe ; he had lost the respect of people and Parliament, and had done much to ensure the ruin of the House of Stuart. He deserved his title, " the wisest fool in Christendom ".

CHARLES I

CHAPTER II

DISPUTE BETWEEN KING AND PARLIAMENT

CHARLES I

THE son who came to the throne in 1625, was a much more attractive man than his father. Charles I was handsome, brave, and the picture of kingly dignity. In private life, he was kind and generous, a good husband and father, a lover of artistic things and a sincere Christian.

There were, however, faults that lay deep beneath this noble surface. Brought up to believe that he ruled by Divine Right, Charles considered himself above the laws made for ordinary men, who were impertinent when they criticised, and treacherous when they opposed him. He broke promises, and was incurably faithless to his friends and enemies, until men came to realise that his word meant nothing.

Yet, to the end, Charles regarded himself as a man of honour who had been smitten by misfortune. Had he been ruthless and direct, he would have won the Civil War. Instead, double-dealing and hesitation brought him to the scaffold.

HENRIETTA MARIA

Charles marries the sister of the King of France

The Spanish Match had failed, so Buckingham, whom Charles adored, hastily arranged a marriage between the King and *Henrietta Maria*, fifteen-year-old sister of the King of France.

The young Queen, a pretty but rather silly girl, was of course a Roman Catholic. She was to grow into a hysterical woman, devoted to her husband, and for ever ready to counsel any plan, no matter how treacherous or ill-advised.

Parliament, called too late to protest, was dismayed at having a Catholic Queen who, they surmised correctly, would bring up children to follow their mother's religion. They were wrong, however, to fear that Charles would turn Catholic.

BUCKINGHAM

War with Spain

The vain and incompetent Buckingham, posing as a Protestant champion, brought about war with Spain (1625). Twelve thousand English foot soldiers, snatched up by the press-gang, were landed on the coast of Holland with orders to march to Germany to help Elizabeth and her husband to win back the Palatine. Buckingham had made no arrangements for feeding the troops or for joining their allies, and the wretched soldiers perished from hunger and disease.

PARLIAMENT DISMISSED

Charles' first Parliament met in an indignant mood. They had been tricked by the French marriage and now were being shamed by the disasters of the war. They refused to grant money until Buckingham was put under control, and until they knew something about the course the war would take. Many of the Members had business interests in America and the West Indies, and they wanted an all-out attack on Spain by sea.

A MARRIAGE WAS ARRANGED BETWEEN CHARLES AND HENRIETTA MARIA, 15-YEAR-OLD SISTER OF THE KING OF FRANCE, LOUIS XIII

The King, furious that they should threaten his beloved friend and criticise his own conduct, dismissed Parliament before they had even voted him the usual Tunnage and Poundage, i.e., the right to collect customs duties on each tun of wine and pound of merchandise.

Parliament dismissed

CADIZ, 1625

Buckingham and Charles now went from bad to worse. A hopeless attack was made on Cadiz with rotten ships and untrained, sickly men. This failure forced Charles to call Parliament again.

The leader of the Commons, *Sir John Eliot*, a squire and Vice-Admiral of Devon, had seen enough of the miserable remnants of the fleet returning to Plymouth to know that Buckingham must be removed. The Members attacked Buckingham with such venom that Charles again sent them home before they had voted a penny.

WAR WITH FRANCE, 1627

As though they had not enough trouble on their hands, Charles and Buckingham next fell into a state of war with France. Charles had promised to favour the Catholics after his marriage, but for the moment he was on bad terms with his young Queen, and had sent her French attendants home. Buckingham, in his usual arrogant manner, quarrelled with the great French minister, Richelieu, over the right to search ships in the Channel.

A MERCHANT SHIP IN THE REIGN OF CHARLES I

War with France

Buckingham himself commanded an expedition to capture the Island of Rhé, which lies off La Rochelle. in the Bay of Biscay. He landed his troops boldly, but the planning was so inept that reinforcements and a fleet never arrived. The French came across from the mainland to slaughter the English at their leisure, and Buckingham got home with fewer than half the 8,000 men he had taken with him.

TYRANNY

In finding the means to wage this useless war, Charles gave the country a taste of what its fate would be under an absolute monarch.

Forced " loans "

A forced loan was issued in every county. Commissioners of Loans, who hated the task, were ordered to obtain " loans " from men of property. Many found reasons for delaying payment, some were let off lightly, others paid under protest and eighty gentlemen went to prison for refusing.

Without system or justice, rogues, poor men and unemployed were pressed into the army, and those soldiers who were not sent to die abroad were billeted on private householders. A penniless rabble rampaged about the countryside, taking what they pleased from house and garden. The indignant owners could get no justice in the law-courts, for the districts were under Martial Law (Army rule).

England, however, was not like France, where the King's officials taxed a down-trodden peasantry. Charles had no permanent civil servants to do his

A PENNILESS RABBLE ROAMED THE COUNTRYSIDE

bidding, but had to rely on the gentry who were Justices of the Peace and Commissioners of Loans. Realising that the King's policy would bring ruin to their own class, the gentry became more and more unwilling to carry out the royal demands. Even Charles could see that he must call Parliament again.

THE PETITION OF RIGHT, 1628

A STUART CHAIR

When Parliament met, its leaders drew up a request, not a demand, that the King should remember the old laws and the rights of Englishmen.

These, they said, were freedom from taxation (i.e., forced loans) without consent of Parliament, freedom from imprisonment without trial, freedom from Martial Law and freedom from billeting of soldiers on private householders. These requests formed *The Petition of Right.* Charles, desperate for money, hesitated and then accepted the Petition. The people who lit bonfires and rang bells for joy at the " victory", did not reflect that a King who believed in his Divine Right to rule, was not likely to keep promises that were forced out of him.

THE DEATH OF BUCKINGHAM

Buckingham had gone down to Portsmouth to take command of another expedition to Rochelle, when a lieutenant named Felton, who had a grudge against the Duke, made his way to his room and killed him with a dagger.

The second attack on Rochelle was another dismal failure, and English ships and troops had become a joke among the professional fighting men of Europe.

Peace with France and Spain

Charles made peace with France, Spain and the German Catholics to give his full attention to his subjects at home.

LAUD

THE BREAK WITH PARLIAMENT

Humiliated in the war abroad, English Protestants became alarmed by the influence of the High Churchmen who circled about the King, flattering him and applying for his advice on all religious matters.

William Laud, Bishop of London, was the most able and energetic of these High Churchmen, who were known as *Arminians*, because they obtained some of their views from a Dutch writer, named Arminius. Laud stood for a disciplined Church of England, for the authority of bishops, for the use of the Prayer Book and ceremony in worship. These practices were hated and suspected by many of the Members of Parliament, who feared that the King, under the influence of his Queen and of Laud, was turning more and more towards Rome.

There was a short session of Parliament in 1629, when the atmosphere was more bitter than ever. The King, as Head of the Church, considered that Parliament was impertinent to put forward its views on religion. The Members, anxious about the King's refusal to respect their right to a share in the government, would not grant Tunnage and Poundage for more than a year. Charles disdained to accept, unless it was for life.

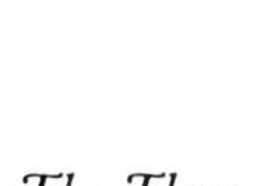

The Three Resolutions

A messenger was sent to dissolve the House, but before he could get in, the Commons resolved to place on record their principles. The Speaker was about to rise to put an end to the discussion, when, amid great excitement, he was held down in his Chair. Sir John Eliot then read out the *Three Resolutions*. These declared that whoever tried to bring in " Popery or Arminianism ", or to alter the Protestant forms of the Church of

THE SPEAKER WAS HELD DOWN IN HIS CHAIR WHILE SIR JOHN ELIOT READ OUT THE THREE RESOLUTIONS

England, whoever collected or paid Tunnage and Poundage without parliamentary consent, was an enemy of the kingdom and " a betrayer of the liberty of England ".

To shouts and cheers, while the Speaker struggled in his Chair and the King's officers hammered on the door, the Three Resolutions were passed. It was the end of Parliament for eleven years.

RULE WITHOUT PARLIAMENT

JOHN HAMPDEN WAS IMPRISONED FOR REFUSING TO PAY THE FORCED LOAN

Charles's methods of raising money

Charles now decided, like his father, to rule without Parliament. His greatest difficulty was to find sufficient money, but he made peace abroad and spent as little as possible at home.

Merchants refused to pay Tunnage and Poundage, and the resistance to forced loans showed that money-raising must appear legal. Lawyers therefore dug out some long-forgotten laws in order to tax the gentry. In medieval times, men holding land worth £40 a year or more, had to serve the King as knights, so their descendants were now fined for having neglected this forgotten duty. All waste land had once been the King's " forest ", but much of it had been under cultivation for centuries. Various landowners were fined as much as ten and twenty thousand pounds for encroaching on royal " forest land " which their ancestors had occupied for generations.

Monopolies were granted to trading companies, but the most famous money-raising device was *Ship Money*. In ancient times, it had been the duty of coastal towns to supply ships for the King's fleet in time of war. Charles demanded ships or money, not only from maritime, but also from inland counties.

The Fleet needed strengthening, for Charles rightly pointed out that pirates were robbing English vessels in the Channel and that sea defence should fall on the whole country. The tax, however, had not been passed by Parliament, and *John Hampden*, a wealthy, much-loved squire of Buckinghamshire, refused to pay. Twelve judges decided against him by seven votes to five, but Hampden's example encouraged others to resist the King in the name of freedom.

Justice was hard to come by when the judges favoured the King's point of view. Eliot and some others of the late Parliament were in prison for failing to apologise for their behaviour in the House. When Eliot fell ill in the Tower, the King refused to release him and, a month later, would not allow his body to be taken home for burial.

Charles revives the Star Chamber

Charles made increasing use of two special courts that had been accepted in former days, but were now the detested instruments of royal tyranny. The *Star Chamber*, a court consisting of the Privy Councillors and the two Chief Justices, could summon any subject and sentence him to imprisonment or fine, without any of the rules of the ordinary law-courts. The

GOSSIPS WERE FORBIDDEN TO USE ST. PAUL'S AS A MEETING-PLACE

A PURITAN

Court of High Commission was hated even more bitterly, for it punished all kinds of religious " offences ", such as the printing of pamphlets and of speaking against bishops and High Church ceremonies.

ARCHBISHOP LAUD

Laud, now Archbishop of Canterbury, was one of the King's most faithful supporters. An able little man, with a sharp eye and sharper tongue, he was determined to silence the Puritans by fines, imprisonment and exile. Much that he did was good. Order and decency were restored to Church of England services, and slack behaviour, such as talking and wearing hats in church, was stopped. The custom of using St. Paul's Cathedral as a meeting-place for gossips and rogues was forbidden. Altars were moved to the east end of churches, and this, in particular, gave great offence to the Puritans.

Through Laud's ceaseless energy, parishes all over the country were inspected and every detail of their services looked into. Books, pamphlets and preachers were banned, and heavy punishment was dealt out to anyone who expressed views contrary to those of the High Church.

Thousands of Puritans go to America

Thousands of Puritans left their homes and made the perilous crossing to America, rather than conform to a method of worship which they felt was wicked. Well-known preachers, such as Prynne, Bastwick and Burton, had their ears cut off and were sentenced to life imprisonment for daring to speak against bishops.

To some, the Puritans appeared to be ridiculous kill-joys, perpetually mouthing the Scriptures and parading their plain dress, pious lives and sour faces. Gloomily preoccupied with a stern God, their harsh religion seemed to penetrate every corner of their lives. But if they were fanatics, it was because Puritans feared sin more than death or banishment.

PEOPLE WHO SPOKE AGAINST THE HIGH CHURCH WERE HEAVILY PUNISHED

Dread of sin made them brave, honest and unyielding. Many were gentry and well-to-do persons of character and education; many were simple workers and countrymen to whom the word of the Bible was more powerful than the commands of a king.

WENTWORTH

If Laud was hated, the King's other chief servant was feared even more. For several years, Thomas Wentworth had been ruling Ireland with such severity that his method of government was known as "Thorough". The Irish, fanatically Catholic, detested their Protestant rulers and the Scottish and English colonists who had been settled on their lands. Though there were powerful Catholic landowners and some Catholic merchants, the bulk of the people lived in poverty and misery, under feudal chiefs who ill-treated their tenants and pillaged their neighbours. Wentworth ruled this unhappy land by the only means that seemed possible, crushing all opposition with iron rule and over-riding the Irish Parliament by the force of his character and will. Men trembled at the thought that "Black Tom Tyrant" might be brought over to England by his royal master.

A PURITAN WOMAN

TROUBLE IN SCOTLAND

The King's rule was unpopular with many of his subjects, but life and business went on much as before, and London, in fact, was extremely prosperous. There seemed no reason why the King should not go on ruling as he pleased until the end of his life. However, he attempted a piece of folly that forced him to call Parliament.

Charles had never lived in Scotland, and he understood little and cared less for its separate government and its devotion to the Presbyterian Church. In 1637, Charles and Laud ordered Scotland to adopt

A PILGRIM FATHERS'
PINE TREE SHILLING

A SIVER WINE CUP, MADE IN 1634

a Prayer Book, based on the English one, in place of Knox's Book of Common Order.

The proud Scots would have none of it. In St. Giles' Church, Edinburgh, a certain Jenny Geddes hurled her stool at the minister's head, and the Town Guard had to be brought to quell the riot that broke out.

All over the Lowlands it was the same. No one would listen to the new service and Scots flocked into the churchyards to sign a *National Covenant*, pledging themselves to defend their religion.

Anyone but Charles would have realised his mistake, but how could he be wrong when he ruled by Divine Right? The Scots must be forced to obey.

THE BISHOPS' WAR, 1639

Charles had no army and no money to hire an efficient force, so he called on the northern nobles to raise their followers.

War against Scotland

A pitiful rabble of ill-armed peasants came reluctantly behind their unwilling lords to face a determined army of Scots, many of whom had seen service in the Protestant armies of Sweden, Holland and Germany. The Covenanters could have massacred the English, but wisely refrained from attack, and a truce was called. For the moment, Charles had to give way and his troops were disbanded.

The King was never able to recognise defeat and he had no intention of yielding graciously to Scottish pride. He sent for Wentworth who hurried over from Ireland, ready to devote his heart and formidable talents to the task of making his royal master an absolute King. Wentworth, created *Earl of Strafford*, proposed to raise two armies, one in Ireland and one in England, and he advised Charles to call Parliament, believing that he would be able to bully it into submission.

THE EARL OF STRAFFORD

JENNY GEDDES WOULD HAVE NONE OF THE NEW PRAYER BOOK, AND HURLED HER STOOL AT THE MINISTER'S HEAD

THE SHORT PARLIAMENT, 1640

After eleven years, Parliament met again and lasted for twenty-three days. It was long enough for the Members to discover that, under John Pym, there was a strong party opposed to the King. Instead of meekly voting taxes for a Scottish war, Pym and his friends voiced their grievances and were angrily dismissed by Charles.

Riots in London

For the first time, riots broke out in and around London. Mobs of apprentices and workmen threatened the life of the Archbishop and hooted at bishops in the streets.

THE SECOND BISHOPS' WAR, 1640

This time, Strafford raised an army by the press-gang. It was a mutinous force that marched north, for the sullen country lads, many of them Puritans, defied their officers, smashed altars in churches and ran away whenever they could.

The Scots, meanwhile, advanced across the border,

captured Newcastle and sat down to wait until they were paid to go home. There was nothing Charles could do, except call Parliament again.

THE LONG PARLIAMENT ELECTED

Pym and Hampden rode about England encouraging men to vote for Puritans, so the new Parliament, when it met, was as determined to make a stand against tyranny as the Short Parliament had been. Most of the Members were the same men, and they came to Westminster to put Strafford down.

Strafford had no fear and no intention of yielding. He meant to stay in the North to train a royalist army, and only came to London at the urgent request of Charles. As a start, he advised Charles to clap the leading Members of Parliament into jail.

Arrest of Strafford

The Commons were too quick for him. Hearing what was afoot, Pym and his supporters drew up an impeachment against Strafford, and carried it to the Lords who would hear the accusation of high treason. Strafford went boldly to the Lords. " I will go," he said, " and look my accusers in the face." But, as he strode to his place, the way was barred and angry shouts arose, " Withdraw ! Withdraw ! " Black Rod arrested him. The King's best soldier and most able administrator was soon to pay the penalty for the insults and fines which two Stuart kings had heaped upon the English nobles.

Strafford went to the Tower. Pym and Hampden conducted the case against him, but, try as they might, they could not prove that the King's chief servant had been guilty of treason. The Commons began to fear that Black Tom might escape, so they passed a Bill of Attainder, simply stating that he had committed offences worthy of death. The Lords passed the Bill and it only required the King's consent to make it an Act of Parliament.

SELLING OLD CLOTHES

JOHN PYM, LEADER OF THE COMMONS

Charles hesitated. On April 23rd, he had written to tell Strafford that he should not suffer in life, honour or fortune. But now, rumours that the royalist officers in the North were plotting to march on London, threw the capital into a panic. A mob surrounded Whitehall, howling all night for Strafford's death. Next day, the rabble increased in size and violence, as fresh crowds came out from the city, inflamed by preachers and Pym's agents. In the old palace, the ladies trembled and wept, priests gave absolution and the Queen hysterically begged her husband to sign. On May 9th, Charles gave way, and betrayed the bravest and most ruthless of his friends.

At first, Strafford could not believe the news. Then he rose from his chair and said aloud, " Put not your trust in Princes." Three days later, blessed by the trembling hands of Laud, who had also been impeached and lodged in the Tower, Strafford went coolly to his death in front of a vast crowd. As the axe fell, a great shout of joy went up. " His head is off ! " cried the mob, and the cry was repeated throughout the countryside.

THE APPROACHING CRISIS

With Strafford dead and Laud in prison, many of the Members felt that enough had been done. The King would surely rule according to custom and the law.

Pym, however, had not finished. Parliament was not to be dissolved without its own consent. Ship Money and all the devices to raise loans and fines were declared illegal. The Star Chamber and the Court of High Commission were abolished. Charles agreed to all.

On religion, however, Parliament was not of

THE TOWER OF LONDON, WHERE STRAFFORD WAS IMPRISONED

one mind. Some Members thought that the Church of England was quite satisfactory, so long as Laud's "Arminian" ideas were dropped; but others wanted the Church entirely remodelled on the Presbyterian system, as in Scotland. Pym and Hampden and their supporters tried to pass a "*Root and Branch Bill*" to abolish archbishops, bishops, archdeacons, deans and canons, but the opposition was so strong that the bill had to be dropped.

ROYALIST LADIES WORE THEIR HAIR IN RINGLETS

All might yet have passed off quietly. Charles appeared willing to sign all that Parliament asked, though he was secretly in touch with Army officers and Catholic agents; he even believed that the Scots would come to his side. He departed for Edinburgh in that hope, leaving Pym and his friends to their religious disputes.

Rebellion in Ireland

Suddenly, news arrived of rebellion in Ireland. Hunger, despair, and religious persecution had caused a terrible explosion of hatred. Four or five thousand Protestants were massacred, and more perished from ill-treatment. Ghastly stories reached England of atrocities committed by the barbarous Irish, and all men agreed that the Catholic rebels must be put down by force. An army must be raised at once, but who would command it?

The answer could not be in doubt. The King commanded the forces of his realm and appointed his officers. If Parliament passed the taxes to raise an army, would not the King use it first to deal with his enemies at home? Pym persuaded the House to pass a Bill, giving the command to "such persons as Parliament can trust."

The Grand Remonstrance

Pym next drew up the *Grand Remonstrance*, a long list of all the King's faults in Church and State since the beginning of his reign. This insulting declaration was meant to show that the King was unfit to choose his councillors or to command his army. It was passed by 159 votes to 148, a majority of only eleven.

A CAVALIER

THE LAST STRAW

Charles arrived home from Scotland in November 1641. He was cheered in the streets of London and went to dine with the Lord Mayor. Men felt that he had come back to keep his promises and to restore the quiet rule of law and custom. A Royalist party had grown up, Parliament was divided, and moderate men began to think that Pym, " King Pym ", as they called him, had over-reached himself.

At Court, Charles was now surrounded by his admirers, led by the handsome, over-confident George Digby. Officers from Strafford's regiments and young bloods ready for any devilment swaggered about full of talk of " blood-letting ". They formed a royal guard and became known as Cavaliers, from the term, " cavaliero ", a Spanish trooper, the brutal foe of Protestants. Their contemptuous label of " Roundheads " for the crop-headed apprentices, was soon to become the popular name for the supporters of Parliament and the Puritan religion.

Roundheads and Cavaliers

The situation in London grew tense. Mobs chanted " No Bishops ! " at Westminster, and the Cavaliers chased them off with drawn swords. In January 1642, the King resolved to arrest the leaders of the House of Commons on charges of high treason. Instead of acting swiftly, he had them impeached in the House of Lords, but did not attempt to make the arrest until the next day.

With 400 armed Cavaliers, Charles went himself to the House to " pull them out by the ears ". But the Five Members, Pym, Hampden, Hazelrigg, Holles and Strode, had already been warned. Pym waited just long enough to make sure that the King would act like a fool, and then tumbled into a boat with the others, to be rowed down the Thames to safety in the City.

MANY ROUNDHEADS HAD THEIR HAIR CROPPED, BUT MOST OF THEM WORE THEIR HAIR LONG, IN THE CURRENT FASHION

Charles entered the silent, horrified House. "Is Mr. Pym here?" he demanded. The Speaker fell on his knees and answered that he could not see or speak but as the House desired. "Tis no matter," said the King, looking hard along the benches, "I think my eyes are as good as another's. All my birds have flown."

This act of folly was the last straw. Men saw that Charles intended to overthrow the rights of Parliament and that all his promises had been given merely to gain time. The Train Bands of London were called out, a Committee of the Commons met in the City, out of range of cavalier swords, sailors came ashore to pledge their support for Parliament, and armed squires rode in from the country.

Charles loses London

A few days later, the King and Queen suddenly left Whitehall for Hampton Court, and then took refuge at Windsor Castle. Although he did not know it, Charles had lost London for ever, and he only returned to his capital as a prisoner.

HAMPTON COURT: WOLSEY'S CLOCK TOWER

CHAPTER 12

THE CIVIL WAR

PRINCE RUPERT, NEPHEW OF CHARLES I

THE FIRST STEPS

The King, who always hesitated at moments of crisis, made up his mind to bring Parliament to its senses. He would send the Queen abroad to obtain money and troops, while he moved to his northern capital at York. Here, he felt sure that his loyal people would support him, and the Scots, he believed, were on his side. After foreign help had been landed at Hull, he would march on London.

In February 1642, the Queen left Dover and was soon in Holland, where she pawned the royal jewels to buy arms, and wrote innumerable letters to the monarchs of Europe. Unfortunately, the King of Denmark, Charles's uncle, was involved in the German wars, the Hollanders were, if anything, on the side of Puritan Parliament, and the French had no intention of interfering unless it suited them. The King's nephew, son of his sister Elizabeth, a spirited young man named Prince Rupert, joined his aunt and worked energetically to raise troops.

Prince Rupert raises troops

Civil war was now certain. The King moved to York and summonded the gentry to his side, but he failed to win over the Puritan Lord Fairfax and his soldier son, Sir Thomas. The Governor of Hull was Sir John Hotham, by no means a convinced Parliament man, and it should have been possible, by skilful management, to persuade him to yield the all-important harbour. The King sent his son to visit the Governor, and then announced that he himself would come to join him. Somehow the chance was bungled, for while Hotham hesitated, the Royalists in the town failed to act. When the King drew near, Hull's gates remained shut and the port was never taken.

Parliamentary support rallies in London

In London, the Train Bands were drilling, and 500 cavalry began to train in Tothill Fields. Puritan preachers urged young men to take up arms for the Lord, and when the Royalist Lord Mayor read the King's Commission of Array, calling all loyal men to the royal service, he was clapped into the Tower.

"KING PYM"

The dogged spirit behind all these preparations was John Pym. Step by step, he had brought about the war, seeing farther ahead than the King and skilfully meeting his every move.

Pym, who had spoken so loudly of privilege and liberty, did not scruple to expel some Members from the House and to have others sent to the Tower. He had used the rabble to bring about Strafford's death, and he used it again to keep London in a ferment. Now that Royalists were quietly leaving the capital, either to join the King or to retire to their estates, he had their houses plundered and their goods confiscated. When the city needed stirring up, there was always some wretched Catholic priest who could be ferreted out and hanged in public.

It was Pym who rigged an election to wreck the authority of the Lord Mayor, and it was Pym who had Philip Skippon, a doughty professional soldier, given command of the Train Bands, making him a freeman of the City only two days before.

Pym understood the use of propaganda. He fostered rumours and demonstrations, and encouraged the issue of innumerable news-sheets to give Parliament's point of view and to keep the City in a fever of

A PIKEMAN OF THE LONDON TRAINED BANDS

indignation. The King's messages from York, offering pardon and peace, were treated with contempt, as perhaps they deserved, but petitions from the King's supporters, of whom there were still some in Parliament, were condemned as "breaches of privilege".

PURITAN PREACHERS URGED YOUNG MEN TO FIGHT IN THE NAME OF THE LORD

PREPARATIONS

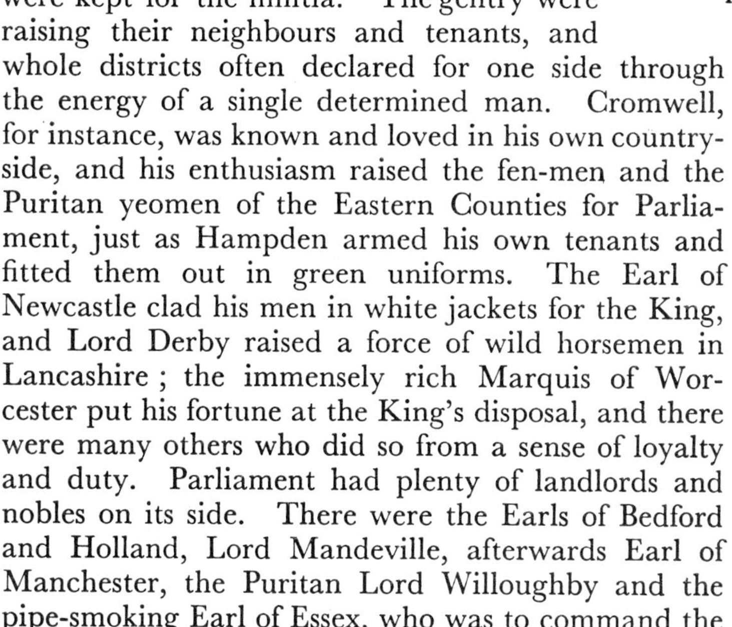

Despite the stream of mild words from York, both sides began to arm. All over the country, arguments took place and blows were struck over the local stores of arms that were kept for the militia. The gentry were raising their neighbours and tenants, and whole districts often declared for one side through the energy of a single determined man. Cromwell, for instance, was known and loved in his own countryside, and his enthusiasm raised the fen-men and the Puritan yeomen of the Eastern Counties for Parliament, just as Hampden armed his own tenants and fitted them out in green uniforms. The Earl of Newcastle clad his men in white jackets for the King, and Lord Derby raised a force of wild horsemen in Lancashire; the immensely rich Marquis of Worcester put his fortune at the King's disposal, and there were many others who did so from a sense of loyalty and duty. Parliament had plenty of landlords and nobles on its side. There were the Earls of Bedford and Holland, Lord Mandeville, afterwards Earl of Manchester, the Puritan Lord Willoughby and the pipe-smoking Earl of Essex, who was to command the first Parliamentary army.

For the moment, the militia was unwilling to be called up, but volunteers and offers of companies and troops of horse flowed in, mostly to the King. It

A LADY OF THE REIGN OF CHARLES I

was evident, however, that the Fleet was Parliament's.

The navy deserts the King

Charles had lost the love of his sea-captains and sailors, not merely because food was bad and pay irregular. They had been reared to detest Spain and Popery, and they hated the King's tenderness towards both. The Lord High Admiral, the Earl of Northumberland, opposed the King, and his Deputy, the Earl of Warwick, a tough and experienced captain, the darling of his crews, secured the Navy for Parliament. Only five captains refused to obey and they were soon rounded up, leaving a few small vessels for the King, and the "Providence" that had carried the Queen abroad.

Without a fleet, the King's plans to receive foreign aid were doomed. He was never able to capture any of the chief sea-ports, except Bristol, and a King of England without a Navy was a sorry figure in the eyes of Europe.

THE WAR BEGINS

In July 1642, fighting broke out in Lancashire, where both sides were recruiting. The Puritan weavers of Manchester resisted a Royalist troop of horse that came to seize the local arms store. Swords clashed and shots were fired. The first man to fall in the war was killed in a wild skirmish that was soon to be repeated in a hundred other towns.

In August, Prince Rupert and his brother Maurice arrived to serve the King. Several counties declared themselves neutral, but all were soon to be drawn into the war.

Charles moved from York into the Midlands with a few hundred supporters and, on August 22nd, hoisted his Standard at Nottingham, calling all loyal men

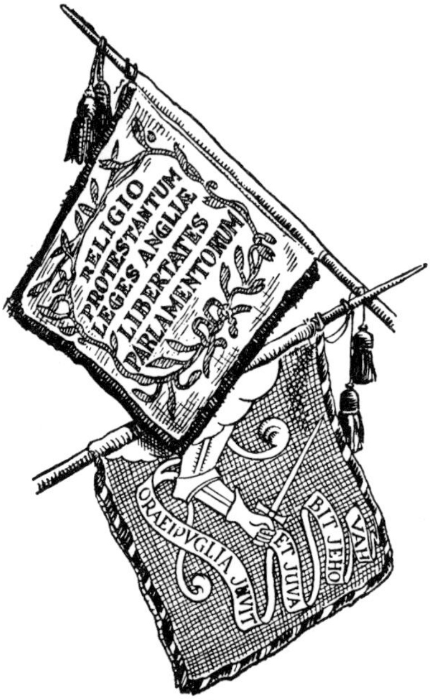

THE ROYALIST AND PARLIAMENTARIAN FLAGS

to arms against the Commons. It was harvest-time, but wet and dismal weather, so, finding few volunteers, Charles marched westwards to gather troops from the loyalist counties along the Welsh border.

THE EARL OF ESSEX

The Puritan Earl of Essex, a veteran of the Dutch wars, left London with an army of half-trained apprentices and undisciplined volunteers, but he showed no resolute intention of getting to grips with the Royalists. In a skirmish at *Powicke Bridge*, near Worcester, Prince Rupert gave the first hint of his brilliant flair for cavalry warfare, but the Cavaliers did not try to hold the city. Parliament's army entered Worcester, sacked the cathedral and smashed its great organ.

Royalists lack a good general

By the middle of October, the King had gathered an army of some 13,000 men, not well-armed but in good heart. Already the difficulties of command were obvious, for there was no outstanding general of Strafford's quality to over-awe the gentlemen volunteers who brought their own troops, and naturally expected to command them. Prince Rupert was made Lieutenant-General of the Horse, but his youth and impatience did not endear him to older commanders.

The royal army moved east, towards London. Essex marched from Worcester to intercept, and the two forces met at *Edgehill* in the centre of England.

AT POWICKE BRIDGE PRINCE RUPERT SHOWED HIS BRILLIANT FLAIR FOR CAVALRY WARFARE

Rupert's well-mounted gentry swept down the slope and scattered the Parliamentary horse opposite. On the left wing, Wilmot was equally successful, but he unaccountably missed some of the Parliamentary cavalry. Thus, when the Royalist infantry advanced to clinch the victory, they were attacked on the flank and had no cavalry left, since the reserves had rashly followed Rupert in headlong pursuit of their flying enemies, and were now plundering the baggage. Then, in the centre, a desperate struggle went on and the Royalist infantry took a severe battering. The Royal Standard was lost, and the King's commander, the Earl of Lindsey, was mortally wounded.

The first battle of the war, Oct. 1642

An onslaught by some of Rupert's returning cavalry saved the day. The Standard was retaken, with Sir Edmund Verney's severed hand still grasping it. As darkness fell, the exhausted armies drew apart, but neither quitted the field.

The King's army had suffered, but Essex had lost much baggage and equipment. His cavalry was scattered, and the Royalists were between him and London. But his army was not destroyed, so, claiming victory, he sent urgently to Westminster to call out every man to defend the capital.

AFTER EDGEHILL

Victory should have been the King's, and the advantage lay with him now.

Cromwell had commanded a troop of horse in this his first battle, and he saw that a little more discipline would have won the day for Charles. He had admired the splendid horsemen on the other side, and remarked to Hampden :

OLIVER CROMWELL

THE BATTLE OF EDGEHILL

A MUSKETEER WEARING A BANDOLIER WHICH HOLDS HIS POWDER. IN HIS RIGHT HAND IS THE REST FOR HIS MUSKET

"Your troops are most of them old decayed serving men and tapsters and such kind of fellows, and their troops gentlemen's sons and persons of quality. Do you think that the spirits of such base and mean fellows will ever be able to encounter gentlemen that have honour and courage and resolution in them?"

Cromwell never forgot what he had seen, nor that the war was almost lost in the first battle. He obtained permission to go back to East Anglia to raise troops who "had the fear of God before them".

The King, as ever, hesitated. He had seen much slaughter and hoped that the battle would bring men to their senses. Instead of allowing Rupert to dash on to London with the cavalry, he made a leisurely advance to *Oxford*, where he set up the royal headquarters.

Essex was therefore able to re-enter the capital. Terror had turned to resolution; earthworks were thrown up, barricades put across the streets, and the Train Bands, under Skippon, drilled with the soldiers.

Royalists approach London

The King advanced to *Brentford*, where Rupert's Cavaliers drove out Parliament's "butchers and dyers", and sacked the little town in rowdy glee. But, nearer London, the Royalists found Essex strongly entrenched among the gardens and orchards with twice as many men. When every cottage, shed and hedge might conceal a dozen musketeers, it would be folly to attack with dare-devil cavalry and ill-armed foot. The Royalists withdrew from *Turnham Green*, and the campaign of 1642 was over.

THE NATURE OF THE WAR

So far, most of the nation was opposed to war. Only in London had there been any enthusiasm to take up arms, and even there, most of the troops were apprentices, unemployed, pressed men, and wild young fellows out for devilment and plunder.

As the war went on, there was no room for neutrals. Every town, shire and village contained some for the King and some for Parliament. Generally speaking, the towns and ports were on Parliament's side, and the country districts, where few understood the quarrel, were loyal to the King. The South and East were mostly for Pym and Cromwell, the North and the West for Charles. But everywhere, there were exceptions. The woollen towns of the North and West Country were full of staunch Puritans, while even in the East, towns like King's Lynn declared for the King. Kent was divided, so were the Midlands and much of the West, where townsmen fought against the Royalist countryfolk. Towns changed hands and changed sides throughout the war, as did the soldiers and some of their officers.

Local engagements

Many castles and fortified houses were put into fighting order, stocked with provisions and garrisoned with troops. Most were royalist strong-points, like Basing House, the great mansion near Winchester that commanded the road to London and the wool traffic. There were Lathom House in Lancashire, where the Countess of Derby defied Fairfax, Brampton Bryan in royalist Herefordshire, Rushall Hall, near Birmingham, Corfe Castle and a hundred more. Sieges and skirmishes went on continuously round these strong-points, though they had little effect on the main

A SKIRMISH BETWEEN ROYALISTS AND ROUNDHEADS

course of the war. Far too many of Charles's supporters were locked up in local campaigns between neighbours.

Money was a problem for both sides, but, in the end, greater for the King. Wealthy landowners, rich Catholics, and Oxford colleges freely gave him their silver plate, jewels and hoards of gold. But when this was spent, there was rarely any more left.

Parliament possessed most of the towns and the centres of trade, where wealth was more likely to be in cash and regular incomes. The merchants who had refused to pay the King's illegal taxes found themselves making " loans " over and over again to Pym.

THE TROOPS

Armies consisted of cavalry, usually gentlemen and freehold farmers riding their own horses, and foot-soldiers, armed with muskets or with sixteen-foot pikes. In a battle, the infantry formed the centre, with the musketeers placed on either side of the pikemen ; each rank fired and wheeled about to the rear of the column to reload, while the next rank stepped forward. A battle was finally decided by " push of pike " in the centre, when the infantry advanced to drive the enemy off the field. The cavalry was stationed on both wings. Where the country was open land, without hedges, cavalry-men were all important, charging with drawn swords and only using their pistols at close range.

Methods of warfare

When cavalry could turn on the infantry, the foot-soldiers were well-nigh helpless, unless, as at Newbury, they had time and discipline to form squares, with the musketeers kneeling under the long pikes. Whenever armies met in enclosed fields or amid gardens, the outcome depended upon the courage of the infantry and their supplies of shot and powder.

In education, equipment and prestige, cavalry were the superior troops, but no campaign could be won by cavalry alone. Charles lost the war because his infantry was insufficiently armed and disciplined to take advantage of the successes won by Rupert's horsemen.

A PIKEMAN

Until the New Model Army arose, regiments on both sides consisted of private companies and troops, supplemented by pressed men of low quality, who often deserted or changed sides. Each side had about 70,000 men under arms, but only at Marston Moor did one army amount to more than 20,000, and then it was a union of three Parliamentary armies. Small campaigns, affrays and sieges went on in various parts of the country, and troops were rarely willing to venture far from their own districts. Gentlemen would join the King for a few weeks when war moved to their shire, but after it had passed, they often went home again.

THE SPIRIT OF THE WAR

Fortunately, the war was not fought with the savagery of continental struggles or of the earlier Wars of the Roses. It was not a class war, nor, in the main, a religious struggle. Fathers and sons were often on opposing sides ; there were relatives in the other camp, and many had sympathies with those they fought. Parliament's Governor of Scarborough said, " I am forced to draw my sword not only against my countrymen but many near friends and allies, some of which I know both to be well affected in religion and lovers of their liberties."

Sir Edmund Verney, a Puritan gentleman, disapproved of much that Charles had done, but in 1642 he wrote, "I have eaten the King's bread and served him nearly thirty years, and will not do so base a

A GENTLEMAN OF THE SEVENTEENTH CENTURY

thing as to forsake him." So Verney died at Edgehill, clutching the Royal Standard. Many a Parliamentarian, too, thought deeply before he took up arms, " I did it not rashly," said one, " but had many an hour and night to seek God, to know my way."

An humane war

Each side accused the other of atrocities, but in truth these were seldom worse than plundering by Cavalier hot-heads and Welsh levies, and the sacking of churches by Puritan fanatics. Roman Catholics were sometimes treated savagely, especially in Lancashire, but usually it was Protestant against Protestant, and there was mercy for prisoners and captured towns. Surrendered garrisons were allowed to march out with their arms and colours. Sometimes prisoners were sent home after an oath never to fight again ; others were offered pay and clothing to change sides.

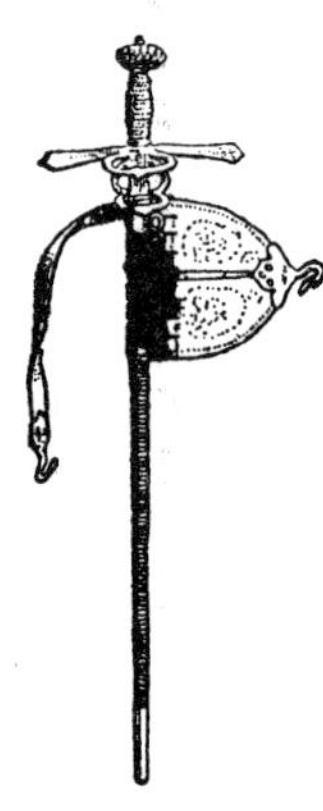

THE KING VICTORIOUS

During the winter that followed Edgehill, the royal cause prospered. Enthusiasm for Parliament had changed to grumbling, expecially in London, where food was dear and trade bad. A peace party arose and, in the City, Royalists took heart. But Pym prepared for war.

The Queen came back and held court at York. Cornish Royalists gave proof of their fighting quality at *Braddock Down*, and West Country loyalists put to sea to challenge Parliament's superiority. Some ships with arms got through from the Continent.

Royalist strategy

The Royalists had a plan to win the war. London was to be captured by a three-pronged attack. The Earl of Newcastle would drive down through the hostile Eastern Association, Sir Ralph Hopton would come from the West to take the Kentish bank of the Thames, and the King, with Rupert, would deliver the knock-out blow from Oxford.

Parliament tried to meet this threat by appointing area commanders. The Earl of Manchester, with Colonel Cromwell, led the troops of the Eastern Association, Lord Grey commanded the Midlands, the Fairfaxes in the North, Sir William Brereton on the Welsh border and Waller in the South. Poor Essex, forever complaining, commanded what was left of the Parliamentary forces.

The King's victories

Through 1643, the King was victorious almost everywhere. John Hampden was killed at *Chalgrove Field* and Rupert's horse went raiding far into the Home Counties. Newcastle defeated the Fairfaxes at *Adwalton Moor*, and drove them into Hull. The

Scale :
1 in.=100 miles

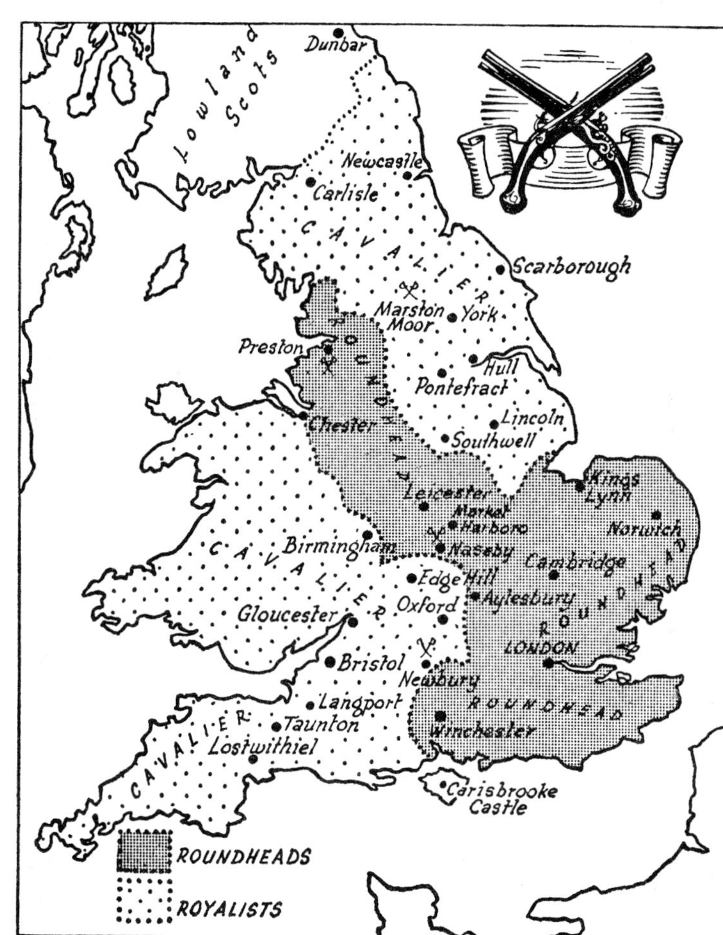

AREAS CONTROLLED BY THE ROYALISTS AND ROUNDHEADS AT THE END OF 1643

Queen was able to move unchallenged across England to Oxford, where she joined Charles on the day that Waller's army was scattered at *Roundway Down.*

Bristol, the second port in the kingdom, was stormed and captured, a dozen West Country towns surrendered, and Royalists rose to arms in Kent. Only Plymouth, Gloucester and Hull held out.

The north and west in the King's hands

Faced with disaster, Pym kept his head. Young Vane was sent to Scotland (by sea, since all the North was lost) to seek an alliance with the Covenanters who dreaded that a Royalist victory would imperil their Church and set loose an invasion by the Irish. The Scots promised to come to Parliament's rescue if England would adopt a Presbyterian form of church government.

Meanwhile, the victorious Royalists advanced into Lincolnshire, where Cromwell was desperately trying to rally the waverers : " Out, instantly, all you can," he commanded. " Raise all your bands ; send them to Huntingdon : get up what volunteers you can ; hasten your horses." Newcastle could have relieved King's Lynn and over-run East Anglia, but his troops were unwilling to march South as long as Hull's garrison could sally out to attack their homes. They returned to besiege Hull.

THE TIDE TURNS

The chance was lost. Cromwell's new cavalry, God-fearing and disciplined, showed their mettle at *Winceby* ; Lincoln was recaptured and Hull relieved.

In the West, Essex got through to save Gloucester, where Colonel Massey, only twenty-three years old, had held out for twenty-three days. Again, the King made a fatal hesitation. Instead of falling upon Essex after he left Gloucester, Charles waited for Irish troops

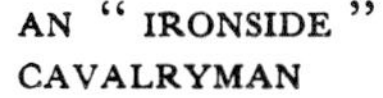

AN " IRONSIDE " CAVALRYMAN

that never came. Racing back to London, Essex extricated his army from a tight corner at *Newbury*, where the Royalists ran out of ammunition when the day was almost won.

Thus, at the end of 1643, when relentless Pym died, the King had won nearly all the victories and had not lost a major battle. But he was no nearer winning the war.

Gloucester and Hull had saved Parliament, but it was the King's lack of good infantry, his failure to concentrate his forces under one supreme commander and his love of secret plans that had failed to clinch victory when the chance was brightest.

AN " IRONSIDE " TROOPER

THE WAR LOST

In 1644, despite Rupert's triumph at *Newark*, the King's cause declined.

The Scots entered England and laid siege to Newcastle ; York was besieged by three armies, and Oxford surrounded. The Queen moved to Exeter, where she almost died giving birth to a daughter. The poor woman, who had not ceased scolding Charles for his scruples about accepting any help, Irish, Spanish or French, was never to see her husband again.

The Battle of Marston Moor

Rupert daringly relieved York, but advanced upon the retreating army and rashly offered battle on *Marston Moor*. Certainly, he expected Newcastle to assist him with greater resolution, but that strange nobleman was piqued by Rupert's lack of tact. The Royalists had 11,000 foot and 7,000 splendid cavalry, devoted to their commander ; the Roundheads had 20,000 foot and 7,000 horse, the best of them led by Cromwell. " Is old Ironsides here ? " enquired Rupert before the battle, and the name stuck.

FIELD GUNS WERE POSTED BETWEEN INFANTRY REGIMENTS AND USED IN THE EARLY STAGES OF A BATTLE

At dusk, neither army had moved, for it seemed too late to fight. Rupert stood down his men and went to supper. Cromwell saw the opportunity and charged. After a furious hand-to-hand struggle, Rupert's cavalry broke: on the other wing, hard-bitten Goring drove Fairfax's horse off the field, while in the centre, the Scottish pikemen fought stubbornly for Parliament until Cromwell could wheel to their support. His flank attack overwhelmed the infantry; the Lancashire Royalists flung down their arms, crying out that they were pressed men, but Newcastle's white-coats fought to the end. Goring's tired cavalry, returning to the field, found that all was over. The King's infantry was destroyed and the North lost, except for a few brave outposts.

Rupert defeated

The effect of this great victory was dimmed by a disaster for Parliament in the West. Essex was trapped at *Lostwithiel* in Cornwall and his army surrendered with 36 cannon and 10,000 muskets, though Essex himself escaped by sea. At the Second Battle of *Newbury*, Lord Manchester failed to defeat the King, returning triumphant to Oxford.

THE NEW MODEL ARMY

These setbacks brought their own remedy. Parliament, now torn by a feud between the Presbyterians and the Independents (who wanted no State Church but complete freedom for Puritan worship), was forced to put its house in order. Cromwell did some plain speaking. The sombre supporter of Pym, hardly known outside his own district, was now a successful commander in the field and a power in the House of Commons. He had lost respect for Manchester and Essex, who, he suspected, would rather have peace with the King than an upset of the

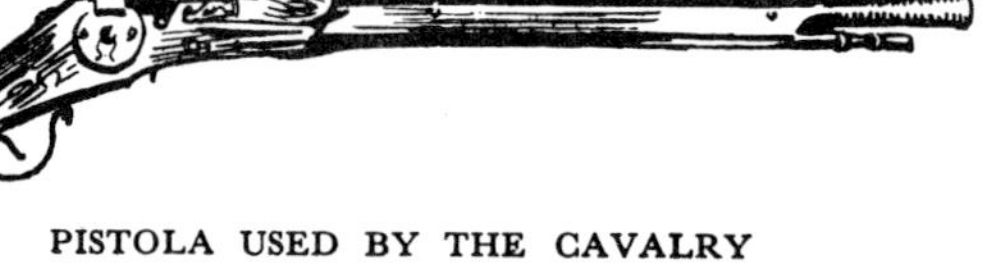
PISTOLA USED BY THE CAVALRY

THE MARQUIS OF MONTROSE

social order, where farmers and tradesmen would be as good as the gentry. The Puritan upper class had not fought Charles for that sort of equality.

After Newbury, however, Cromwell could say, "If the army be not put into another method and the war more vigorously prosecuted, the people can bear it no longer and will enforce you to a dishonourable peace." He had his way. By the *Self-Denying Ordinance*, Members of Parliament were to resign their army commissions: that got rid of Essex and Manchester, and the Earl of Warwick, too. Cromwell himself had to resign from the army, but he was soon reappointed.

The army re-organised

In April 1645, a *New Model Army* came into being to take the place of Train Bands and local forces. It was well-trained, had regular rates of pay and could be moved wherever it was wanted. Sir Thomas Fairfax became the commander-in-chief, with Cromwell as his General of the Horse. For the first time, Parliament had the means to win the war; it had a mobile army whose object was to seek the King and destroy his army in the field, whereas, in the past, the strategy had been to prevent him capturing London.

NASEBY, 1645

Charles, backed by the ever-optimistic Digby, was far from downcast. He held most of the South-West, the Welsh were for him, and the Queen, abroad again, filled him with hopes of aid from France and Holland.

In Scotland, *Montrose* had raised the Highlanders, and from Ireland, there were hopes that *Ormonde* would make a treaty with the rebels and so release troops for England.

Rupert wanted to recover the North and join forces with Montrose, so he moved into the Midlands and captured Leicester, where his Welshmen sacked

the town. Fairfax, drawn away from besieging Oxford, came after the Royalists and offered battle near Market Harborough. For once, Rupert did not want to fight. He was out-numbered, and there was no sign of the drunkard Goring, who should have come up with his cavalry. It was better to continue northwards and to fight when the advantage was clear-cut. Rupert was over-ruled by the King and his confident circle who mocked the New Model Army, calling it the " New Noddle ".

A BLACKJACK, OR DRINKING MUG, AND A WINE BOTTLE

The armies met near the village of *Naseby*, in Northamptonshire. Rupert's cavalry on the right wing routed Ireton's horse and chased them back to the village, where the Prince, remembering Edgehill and Marston Moor, checked the pursuit and returned to the battlefield. Cromwell had allowed Langdale, on the King's left wing, to advance before he launched a counter-attack. The Royalists fought well, but weight of numbers told, and fresh reserves drove them back and then broke them. The King led forward the royal horse guards to restore the situation, when Lord Carnwath seized his bridle and crying, " Will you go upon your death ? " turned the horse's head. Someone thought this movement was a command, and gave the order to wheel right. Before Charles could prevent it, the reserve horse galloped off, carrying him with them.

Royalists defeated at Naseby

This allowed Cromwell to turn the rest of his cavalry on the King's infantry in the centre, where they had pressed hard on Skippon's foot soldiers. The terrible Ironsides broke into the Royalist ranks, and the battle was ending as Rupert returned. His Bluecoats fought to the death, as Newcastle's Whitecoats had done. Once more, the Royalist cavalry escaped, but the infantry was destroyed.

Besides his soldiers, baggage and guns, the King lost his private papers which, Parliament gleefully discovered, proved that he had long been intriguing for foreign help at almost any price.

AFTER NASEBY

The heart had gone out of the King's campaign. He might have gathered up all his garrison troops to join Goring, but he merely moved about feebly along the Welsh border.

Goring was defeated by the New Model Army at *Langport* in Somerset, and Rupert, to save his men, surrendered *Bristol* to Fairfax. The last outposts in the North, Carlisle, Scarborough and Pomfret surrendered, while Cromwell mopped up in the South, where Basing House fell.

Royalists surrender

With the remnants of his cavalry, Charles wandered to and fro. He relieved Hereford, and even penetrated into Puritan Huntingdonshire, and then reached Newark. But there was no plan, only empty hopes, and his mind was poisoned by Digby against Rupert, so that his faithful, tireless nephew was removed from his command and arrested.

During the winter, the Royalists collapsed. Goring escaped to France, and the Prince of Wales to Jersey. Exeter fell, and brave Hopton surrendered and went abroad. Montrose, after his brilliant successes, found that the Scottish Lowlands would not rise for the King : his forces were defeated at *Philiphaugh* and the valiant Marquis fled overseas.

On May 5th 1646, the King left Oxford disguised as a serving-man and, after some faint hope of escaping by sea, gave himself up to the Scottish army encamped at Southwell in Nottinghamshire. The Scots recovered from their astonishment and moved Charles to Newcastle, out of reach of Parliament.

A SIEGE GUN, FOR USE AGAINST FORTIFICATIONS

CHAPTER 13

PARLIAMENT VERSUS ARMY, 1646–1649

THE BROAD-BRIMMED HELMET OF AN ENGLISH PIKEMAN

ALTHOUGH the King had been defeated, everyone, including Cromwell, expected that he would be restored to his throne. What remained to be settled were the terms upon which he and Parliament would again govern the kingdom.

Charles still believed that he would win in the end. His enemies were already at loggerheads, and he thought that he had only to play them off against each other. He expected that the Scots would support a Stuart, but he forgot that they would never give up their Covenant, and also that their army was no match for the New Model Army.

The Scots tried hard to persuade the King to accept the Covenant and establish the Presbyterian Church in England. Although Charles kept the discussions going, he had no intention of agreeing, and was already in touch with Parliament. Finding it impossible to deal with the King, the Scots handed him over to Parliament, and retired across the Border, with £200,000 due to them for the army's pay.

THE KING IN THE HANDS OF PARLIAMENT

Parliament now appeared to have won. The King was a prisoner at Holmby House in Northamptonshire, and all that remained was to disband the army. But this was easier said than done.

The King a prisoner

The root of the trouble was religion. Parliament, judging the whole country by London, was strongly Presbyterian, and showed itself more intolerant than ever Laud had been. Church of England parsons were turned out of their livings, Baptists and other " Godless sectaries " were punished and imprisoned. But the New Model Army was not Presbyterian. Cromwell and his Ironsides were nearly all " Independents ", who disliked the enforcement of official religion by clergymen, whether Anglican or Presbyterian.

The psalm-singing soldiers were not going to be sent home without making sure that their religious views were respected. Moreover, pay was months in arrears, and all that Parliament offered was six weeks' money. Refusing to disband, the soldiers elected " agitators " to put their case to Fairfax and Cromwell.

Cromwell was the only man who was powerful in both Army and Parliament, and, for some time, he did his best to settle the differences. Then he discovered that there was a secret scheme to overcome the Army, to summon the Scots, to call out the Train Bands and to win over the Royalists by bringing Charles to London. Cromwell no longer hesitated. He was now for the Army against Parliament, and he sent a certain Cornet Joyce with 500 horse to fetch the King from Holmby House to some safe place. Joyce, perhaps misunderstanding his orders, took the King to the Army Headquarters at Newmarket.

THE KING WITH THE ARMY, 1647

Charles went cheerfully with his new captors. He was much amused by the turn that things had taken, for Parliament had now been bested by its own Army. Honest men, he felt, would soon come into their own now that the rogues were falling out.

Fairfax, still the senior officer, and Cromwell, led the Army towards London, where plans to resist

A PARTISAN AND A GLAIVE, WEAPONS OF THE SEVENTEENTH CENTURY

collapsed as soon as the terrible red-coats were seen trotting grim-faced into the capital.

The King loses his last chance

The Army generals lodged Charles at Hampton Court and treated him with respect. Their terms for a settlement, called the *Heads of the Proposals*, were more generous than even the King's closest friends could have expected. The Army was to be under control of Parliament for ten years, but then would revert to the King, and complete freedom of worship was to be allowed to all Protestant sects. As one of Charles' advisers said, " never was crown so near lost, so cheaply recovered ".

But Charles would not accept. He went on haggling about the terms, while pursuing secret plans of his own, until the Army chiefs and their men lost patience.

Then came the astounding news that the King had escaped to Carisbrooke Castle in the Isle of Wight, where the Governor was believed to be a Royalist at heart. Charles blundered even here, for the Governor kept him in close confinement and awaited orders.

THE SECOND CIVIL WAR, 1648

Charles was again in touch with the Scots, who promised to send an army if he would accept the Covenant, by which Presbyterianism would be established in England and the Independent sects and the Army suppressed. Royalist risings were to take place all over the country.

When these plans dawned upon Cromwell and the Army, they were bitterly angry. After a solemn

THE BARBICAN OF CARISBROOKE CASTLE TODAY

BRADSHAW, CHIEF JUDGE OF THE COURT OF JUSTICE THAT TRIED CHARLES I

prayer-meeting, they declared that if God gave them victory, they would " call Charles Stuart, that man of blood, to an account ".

The Second Civil War was short and sharp. Wherever they rose, the Royalists were crushed by the New Model Army, and, in the only battle of importance, Cromwell shattered the Scots at *Preston*, though he had less than half their numbers. Charles was taken from Carisbrooke to Hurst Castle, and then to Windsor, while the Army decided what to do with him.

THE KING CONDEMNED

What, indeed, could the Army do with " that man of blood " ? He had never been sincere in his promises to the Scots, he was again in touch with Parliament, and he refused a last offer from the Army ; he said himself in a letter, " the great concession I made this day . . . was made merely in order to escape ".

After the bloodshed of the Second Civil War, Cromwell was certain what must be done. God had given victory to the King's opponents, and that must be a sign that Charles should die. Once convinced that this was God's will, Cromwell carried it through without flinching.

The Rump Parliament

Since the Presbyterians in Parliament were still in favour of dealing with the King, Colonel Pride was sent to the House with a troop of soldiers to allow only Independents to enter. 143 Presbyterian Members were prevented from taking their seats, and the remnant of about 90, known as the *Rump*, voted a special Court of Justice to try the King. *Pride's Purge* left the Army in charge of the country. The Civil War had been fought between King and Parliament : both were defeated.

CHARLES DID NOT DEIGN TO REMOVE HIS HAT IN COURT

The charges brought against the King, and the Court that tried him, were not legal. A free election would have returned a royalist Parliament, for sympathy was running now in favour of Charles, but a small band of men was in power, convinced that they must carry out the Will of God, and none could move them.

Less than half of the 135 men nominated as judges in the Court of Justice attended its sittings. Fairfax himself refused, and when Bradshaw, the chief judge, said that Charles was being tried by the representatives of the people, Lady Fairfax called from the gallery, " It is a lie ! Not half or a quarter of them."

Charles refuses to defend himself

Charles himself, in a dark suit and cloak, did not deign to remove his hat in the court. He held that his judges had no right to try their King and he refused to defend himself. His dignified self-confidence shook his accusers, but the determination of Cromwell bore down the waverers. After four days, Bradshaw donned a scarlet gown and read out the death sentence : ". . . this court doth judge that the said Charles Stuart is a tyrant, traitor, murderer, and public enemy to the good people of this nation, and shall be put to death by the severing of his head from his body ".

FROM THE GALLERY OF THE HOUSE LADY FAIRFAX OBJECTED TO THE KING'S ILLEGAL TRIAL

Three days later, on the 30th of January 1649, Charles asked his servant to bring him a thicker shirt than usual, lest the cold made him tremble as though from fear. He said, " I fear not death. Death is not terrible to me. I bless my God I am prepared."

Execution of Charles I

He stepped calmly through an open window of the Banquet Hall in Whitehall on to a scaffold erected outside. He spoke a few words and knelt down at the block. When the executioner held up the head of the King, the great crowd, kept back by close ranks of soldiers, gave out a groan of despair : " It was such a groan," said a witness, " as I never heard before, and desire I may never hear again."

CHARLES I

CHAPTER 14

(i)

THE COMMONWEALTH

OLIVER CROMWELL

THE King was dead, but none cried, " Long Live the King ", for the Royalists were crushed and the Prince of Wales was a fugitive abroad. Power to make and unmake kings rested with Cromwell and the Army.

In this strange situation, which no one had wanted or foreseen, the generals had to pretend that Parliament ruled the country. But what was Parliament? It was not an assembly representing the people, for most were horrified by the execution of Charles and would have voted for the return of his son. The House of Lords had been abolished; half the original Long Parliament had joined the King, and most of the remainder were dead or had been turned out by Colonel Pride. Everyone knew that the Rump Parliament sat only by permission of the Army.

CROMWELL IN IRELAND

Cromwell President of a Council of State

A Council of State was formed, with Cromwell as its President. The first task must be to restore order in Ireland.

Chaos and bloodshed had reigned there since the rebellion of 1641, but the execution of the King had caused Catholics and Protestants to unite against the Roundheads. All the country, except Dublin and Londonderry, was in the hands of Charles I's friend, the Earl of Ormonde. If Dublin fell, all Ireland would be free from English rule, and then from Ireland the Cavaliers might soon launch attacks on the republic.

Cromwell took the New Model Army to Dublin in August 1649. He had already sent three regiments ahead to strengthen the Roundhead Colonel Jones, and these had trounced Ormonde's army, which now took to its strongholds and fortified towns.

The first siege was at *Drogheda*, near the mouth of the River Boyne. After two assaults had been beaten off, Cromwell himself led the Ironsides into the town. The garrison had refused to surrender and 3,000 were put to the sword, including many priests. A few weeks later the defenders of *Wexford* were also slaughtered without mercy.

SEVENTEENTH-CENTURY ARMOUR: A BREAST-PLATE AND TASSETS

Within six months, despite an illness, Cromwell had subdued most of Ireland. The task was finished by his son-in-law Ireton, who died of fever in 1651, after he had captured Limerick.

Ireland was in a pitiful state. Most of its ravaged countryside lay waste; one third of the population had died from plague, starvation and war, but the English Parliament had no mercy. The lands of the Roman Catholics were seized and given to Cromwell's soldiers, and to men who had lent money to the government. About two-thirds of all Irish lands changed owners in what was called the Cromwellian Settlement.

Cromwell's cruelty in Ireland is an everlasting blot on the name of a great man. Usually he was more tolerant than most people of his time, but to the Irish he showed no Christian pity. His upbringing had made him, like most Englishmen, fear and detest Roman Catholics. Throughout the Civil War, England had shuddered at tales of massacres of Protestants

NO MERCY WAS SHOWN TO THE CAPTURED IRISH

MONTROSE ON HIS WAY TO THE SCAFFOLD

in Ireland, and he and his Ironsides had come to regard the Irish as beyond human compassion. With a terrible sense of religious duty, they slaughtered those who resisted, and gave the others neither hope nor justice.

CROMWELL IN SCOTLAND

In May 1650, Cromwell was recalled from Ireland because a new danger had arisen in Scotland. The Scots were indignant that Parliament, or its Army, had killed the King and had not established Presbyterianism. They now invited young Charles to be King of Scotland, if he would become a Presbyterian. The Prince was far from anxious to accept this religion, but after Montrose had failed to raise the Highlanders and had been taken and executed, Charles no longer had any choice. He agreed to sign the Covenant, and was brought from the Low Countries to Scotland. The Scots then prepared to invade England and put their Presbyterian monarch on the throne.

When Fairfax refused to command an army against his old allies, Cromwell came back as Captain-General to lead his veterans north. He entered Scotland, where David Leslie, commander of the Scots, refused to be drawn into battle. The Ironsides, short of food, exhausted by constant marching, withdrew to Dunbar, where Leslie hemmed them in. They were in a tight corner, when the Scots, urged on by their Ministers, attacked too soon. Cromwell saw his chance and charged, with his magnificent cavalry. On September 3rd 1650, at *Dunbar*, 3,000 Scots were killed and 10,000 captured.

The Battle of Dunbar

This defeat lessened the influence of the Presbyterian ministers, so that Charles, crowned at Scone, was able to take command. While Cromwell occupied

Edinburgh and then moved north, Charles crossed the Border with an army, and marched down through Lancashire towards the western counties.

Charles Stuart defeated at Worcester

Strangely enough, the English Royalists did not flock to the side of young Charles. They disliked the Scots and feared the Ironsides even more. So, when Cromwell came hurrying down from Scotland, he had 30,000 well-seasoned troops against 16,000 Royalists. At *Worcester*, Cromwell's last battle, which he called " God's Crowning Mercy ", the Scots were overwhelmed. Few escaped, but among them was Charles Stuart. After various adventures, " the long dark man, above two yards high ", escaped to France, to wait there in hope of better days.

SEARCH FOR A GOVERNMENT

The burden of leadership now fell upon Oliver Cromwell. His success as a commander, his deep faith in himself as the instrument of God, his force of character and sterling commonsense made him the greatest figure in the country.

He wanted peace and order, with a government of God-fearing men—Puritans of course—but neither he nor anyone else knew what form the government should take, now that the King had been removed. The prime difficulty was that a free election would return a Royalist Parliament to Westminster, yet it was unthinkable that Cromwell and the Army should give away the fruits of victory. They had won because God was on their side, therefore it could not be God's will that the Stuarts should return.

A new Parliament ought to be elected, but the Rump was unwilling to give up its power. At last, Cromwell lost patience. " In plain black clothes with grey worsted

CHARLES ESCAPED TO FRANCE AFTER HIS DEFEAT AT WORCESTER

stockings," he went down to the House and spoke with mounting anger. "You are no parliament," he stormed, "I say you are no parliament. I will put an end to your sitting." Then he turned to Major-General Harrison, "Call them in." Thirty soldiers entered the House and hustled the Members away. On the table was the Mace, symbol of the Speaker's authority. "What shall we do with this bauble?" asked Cromwell. "Here," he said, giving it to a soldier, "take it away."

Cromwell dismisses the Rump Parliament

Charles I had failed to arrest a handful of Members or to overcome Parliament with a show of force; Cromwell had closed the House with such resolution that none cried "Privilege!" this time. "There was not so much as the barking of a dog," he declared afterwards. The Army and its grim-faced commander now held all power in the kingdom.

The Council of Officers decided to summon an assembly of godly persons chosen by the Independent churches. From the list, the Council chose 150. The first name on the list was Praise-God Barebone (Puritans often gave their children names of this kind), so the assembly was scornfully nick-named *Barebone's Parliament.*

This poor little Parliament did not last long. Its Members were good men, but quite unused to politics and practical affairs. Some wanted all kinds

CROMWELL DISMISSES PARLIAMENT

of wonderful changes and reforms, but there was no government. The moderates soon agreed to end their sittings and to give their power back to the man from whom it came.

ADMIRAL ROBERT BLAKE

Thus it was that the Army officers arrived at their *Instrument of Government.* The head of the State was to be a Lord Protector, who would have a Council appointed for life and a Parliament elected for three years.

Cromwell was proclaimed Lord Protector, and in December 1653, nearly five years after the death of Charles I, he took an oath in Westminster Hall. He wore, not uniform, but a black suit, to show that Army rule was over.

(ii)

THE LORD PROTECTOR, 1653–1658

WAR WITH THE DUTCH

One of Cromwell's first tasks was to make peace with the Netherlands. The Rump Parliament had passed the *Navigation Act* (1653), by which goods could be carried to English ports only in English ships, or in the ships of the country from which the goods came, and this blow at the Dutch carrying-trade led to war.

The English fleet was commanded by *Robert Blake*, a Parliamentarian who had done well in the land-fighting but who had little experience of the sea before the age of fifty. In eight major battles, when he was opposed by the great van Tromp, Blake proved himself to be one of our finest admirals.

Honours were fairly even when Cromwell made peace in April 1654. He had never liked the war with

A SAILOR

a Puritan republic, and he wished to set up a great alliance of Protestant powers.

DIFFICULTIES AT HOME

A CHILD OF ABOUT 1660

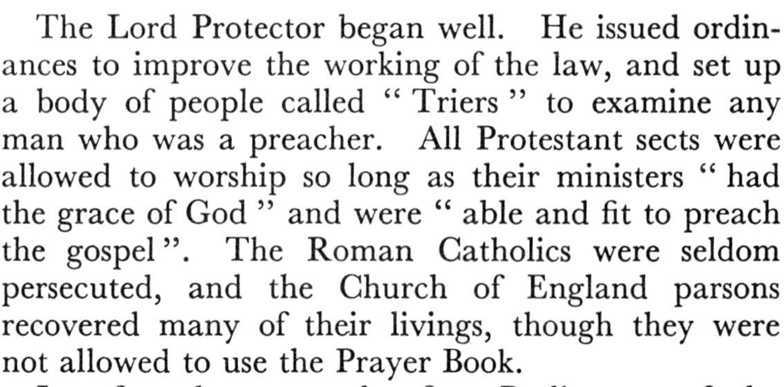

The Lord Protector began well. He issued ordinances to improve the working of the law, and set up a body of people called " Triers " to examine any man who was a preacher. All Protestant sects were allowed to worship so long as their ministers " had the grace of God " and were " able and fit to preach the gospel ". The Roman Catholics were seldom persecuted, and the Church of England parsons recovered many of their livings, though they were not allowed to use the Prayer Book.

In 1654, however, the first Parliament of the Protectorate met, and trouble started. Even Puritans criticised the new form of government, and when Cromwell said they had no right to condemn the Instrument of Government which had brought the new Parliament into existence, the Members retorted that they had more right to be there than he.

Cromwell dissolves Parliament

Cromwell could not have this, and insisted that every Member should accept the Instrument. Those who refused were shut out, but the remainder still criticised and began to talk of reducing the Army. After only five months, Cromwell dissolved Parliament.

By an ironic twist of fate, the Protector found himself ruling as a greater tyrant than Charles had ever dared to be. He collected taxes and dismissed judges who failed to support him in the courts. The Cavaliers, the " Levellers " who wanted an extreme form of republicanism, and other troublesome parties were ground down, and taxes were heavier than ever before, since the Army and Blake's Navy were extremely costly.

In 1655 there were plots and risings which caused

the country to be divided into eleven districts, each under a Major-General, responsible for law and order.

Most of the *Major-Generals* were ardent Puritans, and they forbade every kind of loose behaviour and pleasure-seeking. Sunday was the only day when ordinary folk could relax and enjoy themselves after six long days at work. But in Puritan eyes, Sabbath-breaking was a crime. Dancing, sports, music, play-acting, puppets, bear-baiting and all such " frivolous amusements " were forbidden. Even the inns were closed. The people loathed the Major-Generals, and longed for the good old days when they could enjoy themselves after church.

A PURITAN MAN AND WOMAN

By this time, England was at war with Spain, and Cromwell, like Charles, had to call Parliament to obtain money. In 1656, Parliament met again and, despite the efforts of the Major-Generals to see that only " suitable " members were returned, there was no doubt of the country's feeling. When a special tax on Royalists was proposed, to find the money to pay for the " police " militia, Parliament refused point-blank. Even Cromwell's son-in-law opposed the measure, and the rule of the Major-Generals was over.

CROMWELL'S FOREIGN POLICY

Partly to find occupation for the armed forces, and partly because he wanted a strong England at the head of a Protestant alliance, Cromwell made England respected abroad, as she had never been since Elizabeth's reign.

After peace was made with the Dutch, alliances were formed with Sweden, Denmark and Portugal. Good terms for trade were obtained, as well as promises that no help would be given to the Stuarts.

A PEDLAR

France and Spain were enemies, and since Spain still persecuted English Protestants and refused English merchants the right to trade with her colonies, Cromwell made an alliance with France. He swallowed his dislike of a Roman Catholic country, and the great Cardinal Mazarin overlooked his own feelings about dealing with a republic that had executed its King.

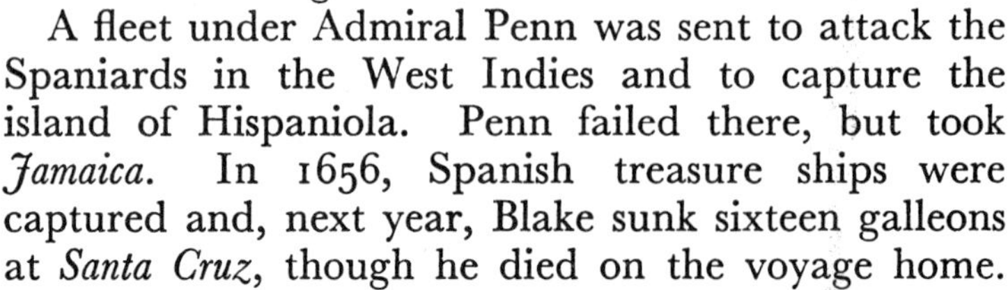

War with Spain

A fleet under Admiral Penn was sent to attack the Spaniards in the West Indies and to capture the island of Hispaniola. Penn failed there, but took *Jamaica.* In 1656, Spanish treasure ships were captured and, next year, Blake sunk sixteen galleons at *Santa Cruz,* though he died on the voyage home.

On shore, Spain was helping Prince Charles to raise troops, so, in alliance with France, Cromwell sent a fleet to blockade the Spanish ports in Flanders, while 6,000 Ironsides went to join the French forces. At the *Battle of the Dunes,* fought in 1658, near Dunkirk, the Ironsides played a major part in the defeat of a Spanish army. *Dunkirk* became an English possession and the Prince's hopes of an invasion were dashed.

A KITCHEN-MAID WALKING ON PATTENS

THE DEATH OF CROMWELL

Alone, Cromwell wrestled with his difficulties. He dealt with unrest in the armed forces, and reduced their size as far as he dared. Civilian plotters, known as the *Fifth Monarchy* men, were crushed, and the Protector seemed more powerful than ever. Yet his power really depended upon his reputation and iron will, and there were signs that his health was giving way.

Even at his greatest, Cromwell had remained a family man, hating to be away from home and forever longing to be at supper with his wife and children. Richard, his elder son, was a country gentleman without ambition, but Harry showed more

CROMWELL'S WIFE

promise and ability. To the anxious father, deeply concerned for his children's religious life, his four daughters were dearest. His favourite, much as he loved them all, was Elizabeth Claypole, whose husband was sourly described as "an ungodly cavalier". She was gay and witty, ready to plead with her father for Royalist prisoners and even to poke fun at the strait-laced Roundheads.

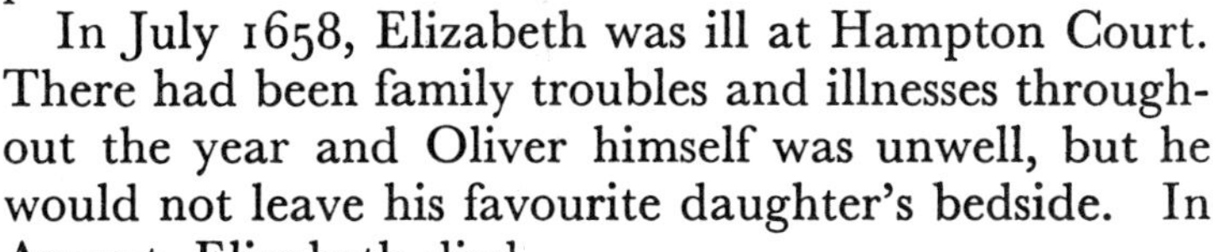

In July 1658, Elizabeth was ill at Hampton Court. There had been family troubles and illnesses throughout the year and Oliver himself was unwell, but he would not leave his favourite daughter's bedside. In August, Elizabeth died.

Cromwell never recovered from his grief. His doctors were puzzled and could do little for him; his body was ill, but worse, he was utterly worn out in mind and spirit.

Cromwell nominates his son to succeed him

He nominated his son Richard to succeed him, and soon afterwards fell into a coma. On September 3rd, the anniversary of his arrival at Drogheda and of his victories at Dunbar and Worcester, Oliver Cromwell died.

TUMBLEDOWN DICK

Richard Cromwell had no wish to be a statesman. He was neither a Puritan nor a soldier, and could not command the support of those who had brought his father to power. He called Parliament, but it contained many enemies of the Protectorate. The Army officers defied him and clearly intended to limit his power, so, with great common-sense, Richard threw up his post and retired into private life.

THE END OF THE COMMONWEALTH

The Army officers, caught unawares by Richard's abdication, recalled the Rump Parliament, quarrelled

A CROMWELLIAN CLOCK

with it and expelled it. The country was on the verge of revolt, and everyone looked for a leader who would restore the kind of government that Englishmen understood. Even Presbyterians and Independents were coming to see that King, Lords and Commons must be brought back, provided there was no persecution of Puritans and no ruling without Parliament.

A leader appeared in the person of General Monk, commander of the Army in Scotland. He had never taken sides violently, and was not one of the little group of officers who were struggling for power.

With the approval of the Scots and an army at his back, General Monk marched towards London. The generals, who might have opposed him with force, found that even the New Model Army did not want war again, and it is to their credit that they laid down their power when they saw that the people wanted a peaceful settlement.

New Parliament recalls Charles II

Monk called together the surviving members of the Long Parliament and persuaded them to dissolve themselves. Then a new Parliament invited Charles II to return from Holland on conditions known as the *Declaration of Breda.*

On the 25th of May, 1660, Charles II landed at Dover. As the King rode through Kent, the people shouted and cheered, decked their houses with garlands and ribbons, and strewed the way with flowers. In London, the walls were hung with carpets and tapestry, bells and trumpets pealed out and the fountains of the city ran with wine.

GLASS GOBLETS OF THE SEVENTEENTH CENTURY

CHAPTER 15

KING CHARLES II

1660–1683

CHARLES II

On the day of his joyous entry into the capital, Charles II was thirty years old. With his curling hair, dark complexion and thick lips, he looked more like a foreigner than an Englishman, though his affable manner and love of sport endeared him to ordinary men. No matter how late the revels at Court, he might be seen soon after dawn sailing on the Thames, riding or hawking in the parks, or striding at tremendous speed across country. He was interested in science, navigation, architecture and ships. His careless charm concealed great intelligence, but he was utterly lazy.

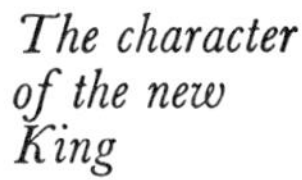

The character of the new King

Years of living in foreign courts, often almost penniless, among vicious companions, had taught him that an easy smile and a witty tongue could see a man through all manner of difficulties. Charles preferred pretty women and rowdy company to sober statesmen, and the French way of life to English notions of liberty. He would rather be a king than a fugitive, and he had no intention of going either to the scaffold or on his " travels " again.

Beneath this affable, idle manner, Charles was at heart a Catholic and an absolute monarch. He intended to rule without Parliament if that was possible, and to restore the religion of Rome when the time was ripe. For the moment, he meant to enjoy himself.

THE SETTLEMENT

The King's chief minister was his father's old adviser, *Lord Clarendon*, who did his best to put the kingdom to rights.

A CROWN PIECE OF THE REIGN OF CHARLES II

A LADY AND GENTLEMAN IN THE REIGN OF CHARLES II

The bodies of Cromwell, Ireton and Bradshaw were dug up and hanged at Tyburn for all to see, but, apart from the "regicides", i.e., those who had condemned Charles I, there was pardon for everyone. The Army red-coats drew their full pay and went home to their shops and farms. In Scotland, there was no trouble, for the execution of Argyll seemed a small price to pay for a return to independence.

Some of the Cavaliers, it was true, complained loud and long. Those who had suffered exile and confiscation of estates recovered most of their property, but many who had been forced to sell whole parcels of land to pay Parliament's fines, never regained their own. This was part of the agreement that brought Charles II to his throne, and many a brave, ruined Cavalier could only lament the ingratitude of kings.

Parliament next proceeded to crush the Puritans. By a series of laws, known rather unfairly as the *Clarendon Code*, all members of the various Puritan sects were barred from positions of responsibility. Some 2,000 Puritan clergy were expelled from their livings. Anyone attending a religious meeting, except of the Anglican Church, was to be punished by imprisonment and then by exile. No clergyman or schoolmaster was allowed to come within five miles of a town, unless he declared that he would never attempt "any alteration either in Church or State".

The Clarendon Code

The Clarendon Code made it impossible for Puritans to hold any office, such as town councillor, magistrate or Member of Parliament, or to educate their children beyond the level of the humblest village school. Hitherto, many men of breeding and importance, including Essex, Bedford and Hampden, had been

Puritans, but, from now on, the gentry obeyed the new laws and attended their parish churches. With few exceptions, the Dissenters or Nonconformists were working-class folk. Those who clung obstinately to their Puritan religion were weavers and dyers, small tradesmen, labourers in the fields and even tinkers, like John Bunyan, who spent more than twelve years in Bedford jail. His immortal " Pilgrim's Progress " expressed the passionate faith and upward-gazing zeal of humble people reaching out for God.

" The Pilgrim's Progress "

BEDFORD JAIL, WHERE BUNYAN WROTE " PILGRIM'S PROGRESS "

THREE DISASTERS

In 1664, the *Second Dutch War* broke out, for much the same reasons as in Cromwell's time. At first, the English Navy, to which the King and his brother James, Duke of York, were devoted, had rather the better of things. James, as commander of the Fleet, won a victory off *Lowestoft*, but the Dutch recovered and struck back hard. In 1667, when some of our ships were laid up for economy, Admiral De Ruyter sailed into the Medway to destroy several warships at *Chatham.*

The nation was filled with anger and shame at this humiliation, though England did reasonably well out of the *Treaty of Breda* (1667) that ended the war soon afterwards. The trouble was that Parliament

JOHN BUNYAN

SAMUEL PEPYS

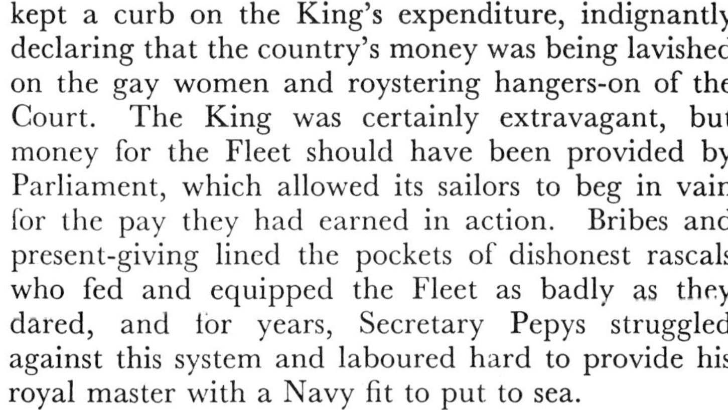

kept a curb on the King's expenditure, indignantly declaring that the country's money was being lavished on the gay women and roystering hangers-on of the Court. The King was certainly extravagant, but money for the Fleet should have been provided by Parliament, which allowed its sailors to beg in vain for the pay they had earned in action. Bribes and present-giving lined the pockets of dishonest rascals who fed and equipped the Fleet as badly as they dared, and for years, Secretary Pepys struggled against this system and laboured hard to provide his royal master with a Navy fit to put to sea.

The Plague in London, 1665

Before the Dutch attack on Chatham, London had suffered two other catastrophies that made men wonder if God was visiting them with vengeance for the wickedness of the Court and their own return to ungodly amusements. In 1665, an outbreak of bubonic plague brought life in the capital to a standstill. Severe visitations of *Plague* had occurred in England ever since the Black Death, and there had been sharp attacks in the reign of James I, when 30,000 died, and Charles I's time thirty years before. This outbreak, which was to be the last, filled people with intense fear, partly because of the greater comfort and security in which many of them now lived, and partly because the size of the population caused the problems of treatment, collection and burial of the dead to be almost insoluble.

All who could, fled from the city. "Lord, how empty the streets are," wrote Pepys in his diary, " . . . and they tell me that in Westminster, there is never a physician left, all being dead."

IN 1665 THERE WAS A TERRIBLE OUTBREAK OF PLAGUE IN LONDON

THE GREAT FIRE OF 1666 BROKE OUT IN PUDDING LANE

When the winter came on, the Plague lessened and died away, but a year later, in 1666, the *Great Fire* broke out in Pudding Lane and raged for five days. The whole of the city, between the Tower and the Temple—the prosperous business and residential area—was destroyed, but it is not true to say that the Fire swept away the verminous and stinking hovels in which the Plague was bred. Many old and dilapidated buildings were burned down in the City, but the slums of the poor were in the " Liberties " outside the walls, and these were hardly touched by the fire.

The Great Fire, 1666

In popular imagination, the Fire was the work of Catholics, and men hourly expected a French invasion. Commonsense soon reasserted itself, and the well-to-do merchants set to work to rebuild in brick and stone, while Christopher Wren, his plans for a

TO PROTECT THEMSELVES AGAINST THE PLAGUE, DOCTORS WORE A MASK STUFFED WITH HERBS, A LEATHER TUNIC, A HOOD AND GLOVES

THE SPIRE OF ST. MARY LE BOW, A CHURCH BUILT BY WREN

noble capital disregarded, applied his genius to replacing the churches and calculating the details for a new St. Paul's.

France had recovered from the religious struggles between Catholics and Huguenots, and was now the chief nation in Europe. Under two great ministers, Cardinals Richelieu and Mazarin, a strong central government ruled the country untroubled by any assembly like the English House of Commons.

Mazarin died in 1661, and Louis XIV began his long era of autocratic power. Near Paris, the great palace of Versailles was built to provide a setting for the gorgeous monarch whose Court was the envy of every prince in Europe.

All the wealth of France, squeezed from her toiling peasants, flowed to Versailles. In its marble and mirrored halls, Louis reigned supreme, amid his courtiers, ladies, engineers and artists, who waited upon him with such extravagant ceremony and adoration that he was called " le roi soleil ", the Sun King.

While the Court basked in his brilliance, Louis planned to extend the frontiers of France to the Rhine. His invasion of the Spanish Netherlands so alarmed the Dutch that, seeing themselves as the next victims, they made an alliance with Sweden and with their late enemy, England. This *Triple Alliance* (1668) of Protestant nations halted the French plans, but Louis countered by buying off Sweden and Charles II.

THE SECRET TREATY OF DOVER

Charles was partly French, and everything about France attracted him—her hospitality during his exile, her wealth and splendour and religion.

LOUIS XIV

THE EARL OF SHAFTESBURY

By the *Treaty of Dover* (1670), France was to pay for a war against Holland ; England would lend her fleet, and the conquered country would be divided. In a second secret treaty, Louis promised to pay Charles an income if he would grant freedom to Catholics and establish their religion with the help of French troops.

By all the rules of war, little Holland should now have been crushed. But at sea, the Dutch proved a match for the English. On land, they checked the French armies by flooding their own countryside. De Witt, leader of the republican party, was murdered in 1672 and young William of Orange became Stadholder of the United Provinces. William was the husband of Mary, Protestant daughter of James, Duke of York.

WHIGS AND TORIES

The Test Act, 1673

Charles, who had long concealed his political cleverness under a pose of easy-going laziness, seemed to be baulked. The French money had run out and his *Declaration of Indulgence* (1672) giving freedom of worship to Dissenters and Catholics, raised a storm of anti-Catholic hatred. The Dissenters would not accept religious liberty if it was also given to Papists, and Charles had to agree to the *Test Act*, which compelled persons in official positions to declare their disbelief in the Catholic faith.

Opposition to the King was led by Ashley, *Earl of Shaftesbury*, a former minister who was enraged by having been tricked over the Treaty of Dover. He formed a " Country Party ", which became known as *Whigs*, from the name for Scottish Covenanters. The King's friends were the " Court Party ", nicknamed *Tories*, after some violent Irish outlaws.

Charles' difficulties were increased by the fact that he had no legitimate son to succeed to the throne.

CATHERINE OF BRAGANZA

Early in his reign, he had married a Portuguese princess, Catherine of Braganza, whose dowry included Tangier and Bombay. Spurned and ridiculed by the King and his magnificent ladies, unhappy little Catherine had her revenge, for she produced no royal children for the Stuarts. This meant that the King's brother, an avowed Catholic, was heir to the throne.

TITUS OATES AND THE POPISH PLOT

In 1678, a loathsome character named Titus Oates appeared from France with a story of a Popish Plot to murder the King, to set James on the throne and enforce the Catholic religion. This " sorry, foul-mouthed wretch ", denounced the Duke's secretary, Coleman, whose rooms were found to contain some highly suspicious papers. Then a popular magistrate, Sir Edmund Berry, before whom Oates had sworn his tale, was waylaid and murdered.

Persecution of the Catholics

These happenings roused London to panic-stricken fury. Peaceful Catholics and innocent citizens were dragged to prison and execution, while Oates, hurling accusations left and right, was the hero of the hour. The King, too clever to be deceived by the uproar, did nothing to save the Catholics, lest his own secrets were uncovered. Meanwhile, the venomous Shaftesbury, with his " brisk boys " beating up the Catholics, organised an election campaign from his " Green Ribbon Club " in Chancery Lane. A Whig Parliament was returned and at once proposed an *Exclusion Bill* to keep James from the throne. Charles, faithful to his own family, would have none of this ; so, sending James out of the country for a time, he dissolved Parliament.

CATHOLICS WERE ATTACKED IN THE STREETS BY SHAFTESBURY'S " BRISK BOYS "

Shortage of money soon compelled Charles to summon another Parliament, this time at Oxford (1681), away from the mob that had overwhelmed his father. Here, Shaftesbury made a fatal mistake. The Whigs proposed that the succession should go to the *Duke of Monmouth*, a handsome Protestant youth, who was the illegitimate son of Charles and Lucy Waters, one of the King's early loves.

The Duke of Monmouth

THE KING'S TRIUMPH

At this tense moment, Charles showed nerve and a clear head. He realised that the anti-Catholic fury was dying down, and that juries were refusing to convict on Oates's vile accusations. Louis XIV made an offer of three years' income, paid in gold without even a receipt, and Charles knew that he was saved.

In a sedan chair, he went to the House of Lords. From a second, curtained chair, were produced the Robes of State which he must wear for this occasion, and with smiling suddenness, Charles dismissed Parliament.

Charles dismisses Parliament

Unlike Pym's men in 1642, the Whigs were totally unprepared, with no plan to resist or to continue sitting. While Shaftesbury tried desperately to rally them, they dispersed in a panic, riding hard for their homes, before the triumphant Tories could take vengeance.

Shaftesbury fled to Holland and died there in misery, but a few desperate members of the Green Ribbon Club, with one or two old Cromwellians, hatched a plot to kill the King at Rye House, on the way from Newmarket. The *Rye House*

RYE HOUSE, WHERE A PLOT TO KILL THE KING WAS DISCOVERED

Plot was uncovered, and two of the leaders, Lord Russell and Algernon Sidney, were executed.

The country, sick of the whole business, took Charles back to its heart. For his last four years, the King drew his income from France and ruled as he pleased. He dared not introduce Roman Catholicism. Events had shown him how deeply that religion was detested, and he knew that his Tory supporters, strong in their persecution of Dissenters, would never allow him to be a Catholic king.

Death of Charles II, Feb. 1685

Only on his death-bed did Charles admit his religion. James whispered in his ear and the King answered very loud, " Yes, with all my heart." A priest was sent for, who turned out to be the same who had helped him to escape from Worcester. The room was cleared, and the old priest gave the dying man the last rites of the Catholic religion.

Soon afterwards, Charles apologised to the bystanders for taking so long in dying. So he died, as he had lived, with a jest for the world about him, but with the Catholic faith in his heart.

SEDAN CHAIRS WERE OFTEN USED IN LONDON'S MUDDY STREETS

CHAPTER 16

THE LAST STUART KING

A CORONATION MEDAL STAMPED WITH THE HEAD OF JAMES II

JAMES II came to the throne with more power than any Stuart before him. In Parliament, the Tories, falling over themselves to express their loyalty, voted him a sufficient income for life. His brother had somehow collected a small standing army, which he was soon able to increase, and, across the Channel, the great French king was his faithful friend.

There was one great misunderstanding from the start. James had promised to maintain the Church of England, and men believed that he would keep his own religion to himself. On his side, James believed that the zeal with which High Churchmen hunted down the Nonconformists, proved them to be halfway towards Catholicism. Monarch and Tories quite misjudged each other.

MONMOUTH'S REBELLION

THE DUKE OF MONMOUTH

The tragic event that led to James's ruin was an ill-starred attempt to put Monmouth on the throne. Exiled Whigs in Holland planned a two-fold rebellion, one rising in the Puritan South-West and a second in Scotland.

The Earl of Argyll, son of the old Covenanter, found no support in Scotland and was captured and executed, but Monmouth landed at Lyme Regis and very soon had an army behind him. The West Country peasants saw in the handsome youth a Protestant hero who would rescue them from persecution.

At Taunton, Monmouth was proclaimed King, but his brave country lads were armed only with rusty

A POWDER-HORN

swords and old muskets for which they had little powder and shot. Some had tied to poles the scythe blades that they snatched from barn or outhouse. Against this pathetic army marched a force of trained soldiers, commanded by Lord Feversham and a promising officer named John Churchill.

The rebels made a night attack on the royal army at *Sedgemoor*, where surprise and desperate courage almost succeeded but, at dawn, their ammunition spent, they broke and fled across the Somerset plain. The regular troops rode them down, killing hundreds, rounding up prisoners and hanging them by the score. Monmouth himself was taken, half-dead in a ditch, and his grovelling tears won no mercy from his uncle.

The miserable story did not end there. Lord Chief Justice Jeffreys was sent down to the West to try the rebels in the crowded jails. At the *Bloody Assize*, he bullied and raved at his victims with a ferocious delight that amounted to madness. In four weeks, he sentenced over 300 persons to death, including a woman who had merely given food to a few exhausted fugitives. 900 others were transported to the plantations of the West Indies.

The Bloody Assize, 1685

JAMES THE TYRANT

The ease with which the rebellion had been crushed convinced James that he now could put through his own policy.

The army, largely officered by Catholics, was increased to 30,000 men, nearly half of them in a great camp at Hounslow Heath, where their ruthless behaviour was meant to overawe the

THE PATHETIC ILL-EQUIPPED ARMY RAISED BY THE DUKE OF MONMOUTH

JUSTICE JEFFREYS BULLIED HIS VICTIMS WITH A FEROCIOUS DELIGHT THAT AMOUNTED ALMOST TO MADNESS

Londoners. But, apart from their officers, the hard-bitten troops were Protestants, and only in Ireland was James able to recruit Catholic soldiers.

Everywhere, Catholics were appointed to official positions, though the Test Act still existed. At Oxford, a royalist town, the Fellows of Magdalen were driven out for refusing to have a Catholic Head of their College. Staunch Tories on the Council were replaced merely because they were Protestants, and vacant bishoprics were left empty or filled by men who were instructed " to bring round " the clergy. The squires and parsons who had given their support to the King began to realise that power was passing into Catholic hands. Thus, when James tried to have the Test Act repealed, his docile Parliament refused and was promptly dismissed.

Power in the hands of the Catholics

The King then announced that he could " dispense " with any Act of Parliament. Judges who upheld the law were removed from their posts.

THE SEVEN BISHOPS

Suddenly, James sought the favour of the Dissenters. This astonishing move arose from his need to find support on the town councils and in a new Parliament, when he realised that the High Church Tories were not going to turn Catholic. James therefore offered toleration to the Dissenters and an end to all religious tests.

The Dissenters might dislike the Church of England parsons, but they feared the Catholics still more. With a mixture of nobility and common-sense, the Dissenters refused to accept the *Declaration of Indulgence.*

James remained blind. In April 1688, he ordered the Declaration of Indulgence to be read in all churches. The Archbishop of Canterbury and six of his bishops protested, and were placed in the Tower on a charge of seditious libel. All England followed their trial with bated breath. " The concern of the people for them was wonderful," said an eye-witness, " infinite crowds were in their houses praying for the bishops as they passed out to the barge along the Tower wharf ".

JAMES II'S PROTESTANT DAUGHTER, MARY

A jury found the Seven Bishops " Not Guilty ". That night, London was ablaze with bonfires, and in hundreds of windows stood a row of seven candles, the middle one taller than the rest. On that same night, some of the leading men in the country sent a letter to William of Orange, inviting him to come across to England to save the Constitution and the Protestant Church.

THE END OF JAMES II

Just before the trial of the bishops, James' second wife, an Italian princess, had given birth to a son. It was this event that caused the letter to be written, for while James had no son, the heir to the throne was his Protestant daughter, Mary, wife of William of Orange. Men had felt that they could wait for James to die, but now that a son had been born, they must act or accept a line of Catholic kings on the English throne.

William could not have left his beloved Holland if Louis XIV had made a move towards the Netherlands. But Louis, whose ambitions had united the Protestant and Catholic powers of Europe, sent his armies to attack the Holy Roman Emperor across the Rhine. The coast was clear for William.

A SOLDIER AT THE TIME OF THE " GLORIOUS REVOLUTION "

On November 5th 1688, an army of Dutch and Danish soldiers landed in Torbay. With his banner proclaiming " A Free Parliament and the Protestant Religion ", William moved cautiously inland, taking great care to give no offence.

James advanced towards Salisbury, but his army, apart from the Irish troops, was so unreliable that he drew back towards London. At this moment, his best and favourite general, whom he had made Lord Churchill, left him and rode into William's camp. The King reached London to hear that his daughter Anne, aided by Lady Churchill, had also fled.

Yet, so strong was the Tory feeling of loyalty, that the day might still have been saved if James had stood his ground and promised to rule according to the wishes of his people. But, as William's army drew nearer, the King's nerve failed. He sent the Queen and his baby son to France, and, next day, fled with only a handful of supporters. He was captured at Faversham and brought back to the capital where his presence was so embarrassing that he was allowed to escape again. As he was rowed down the Thames in a small boat, the Great Seal, needed for all official documents, was dropped into the river.

With that feeble gesture of defiance, the last Stuart king went into exile, to die in a French palace given him by Louis XIV. Without a blow being struck, the *Glorious Revolution* had brought the old style of monarchy to an end.

WILLIAM OF ORANGE

CAPTAIN JOHN SMITH

CHAPTER 17

ENGLISHMEN ABROAD

When Queen Elizabeth died in 1603, there was no permanent settlement in America where Englishmen could set up home. Raleigh's plans had failed, but in 1607, a party of about 100 settlers made a fresh start in *Virginia*, where they built a fort named Jamestown, after the King. Through the energy and courage of their leader, Captain John Smith, the tiny colony survived hunger, despair and attacks by Red Indians.

EARLY TOBACCO PIPES

The discovery that tobacco flourished in Virginia's rich soil saved the colony. Despite James I, the smoking habit spread rapidly in western Europe, and the settlers were able to sell all the tobacco they could grow. Younger sons of the gentry, accompanied by the sons of their fathers' labourers, went out to take up grants of land, and to build themselves fine houses from which they presided over estates stretching for thousands of acres. Thus, Virginia came to be peopled by a royalist aristocracy, whose servants were soon to be reinforced by black slaves. Most of the settlers went willingly in hope of " bettering " themselves ; the Government sent out convicts and, later on, prisoners of the Civil War.

Carolina, lying south of Virginia, was founded in 1663. Named after Charles II, like its chief town, Charleston, its climate and soil caused it to develop the same kind of society as Virginia, but here, the main crop was cotton, and this, too, required slave labour.

THE " MAYFLOWER "

Meanwhile, a colony, different in spirit and religion from Virginia and Carolina, was struggling to its feet in the north. In 1620, after an attempt to found a community in Holland, a body of 102 Puritans known as "Separatists", left Plymouth in the *Mayflower*. A fearsome voyage brought them, not to the shores of Virginia, but to a northerly bay enclosed by Cape Cod. In thankfulness for their deliverance from the sea, the "Pilgrims", as they called themselves, decided to build their homes on this bleak coast.

Between 1628 and 1640, Laud's persecution brought 20,000 more Puritans to *Massachusetts* to join the original *Pilgrim Fathers*. They were the best type of Englishmen, yeomen, small gentry and craftsmen, mostly from East Anglia, where Puritanism and hard work went hand in hand with a spirit of independence and neighbourliness. Helped by merchant brethren at home, their trade grew, and Boston, the chief town, rapidly became a merchant city, bustling with prosperity and self-importance.

Separate colonies, New Hampshire, Connecticut (1635) and Rhode Island (1636), branched off from the first settlement.

Scale: 1 in. = 250 miles

BRITAIN'S COLONIES IN NORTH AMERICA

A COLONIAL FARMHOUSE

These colonies, known together as *New England*, formed a kind of Bible Commonwealth, whose "Church members" were so rigidly Puritan that they allowed even less toleration than they had known at home.

Maryland, originally part of Virginia, was granted to Lord Baltimore in 1632, and named after Queen Henrietta Maria. It was meant to be a colony for Roman Catholics, who were shut out from the other settlements, but English Catholics, despite persecution, did not emigrate in large numbers, and Maryland became mainly Puritan.

England acquires Dutch settlements in America

Between New England and Virginia, lay some Dutch settlements known as the New Netherlands. When England and Holland made peace at the Treaty of Breda (1667), England acquired Delaware, New Jersey and New Amsterdam, which was re-christened *New York*, in honour of James, Duke of York, admiral of the Fleet. At first, no one had a high opinion of these American gains, but they were to prove immensely important. With Maryland and Pennsylvania, they were known as the *Middle Colonies*, soon to be peopled by immigrants from Protestant Europe, from England, where the Quakers were driven out by the Clarendon Code, and from New England where the intolerant "Church members" were all-powerful. The Dutch settlers accepted British rule because of the tactful wisdom of Governor Nicolls.

THE QUAKERS TRADED FAIRLY WITH THE INDIANS

RENÉ DE LA SALLE

In 1680, Charles II granted *Pennsylvania* to William Penn, a prominent Quaker, who encouraged persecuted " Friends " to make their homes there. The name of the colony's chief town, Philadelphia, means " brotherly love ", and the earnest Quakers, unlike most settlers, set a new standard of decency in trading fairly with the Indians.

Thus, when James II fled from his kingdom, there was a long strip of English territory stretching from New England all down the eastern coast of America to the borders of Spanish Florida in the south. In less than 80 years, through accident, determination, Royal grants and treaty, this beginning of an empire was firmly established.

THE FRENCH IN NORTH AMERICA

French Colonies in North America

While the British were settling along the American seaboard, Frenchmen took possession of New France, the land that is now Canada. They sailed up the St. Lawrence river and explored the land on either bank and the Great Lakes. Champlain founded the cities of Quebec and Montreal, and, in 1682, La Salle sailed down the Mississippi and reached the Gulf of Mexico. At the river mouth, he set up a cross to claim for France all the land through which he had travelled. It was named *Louisiana*, after King Louis XIV.

The French colonies were different from the English. Whereas the Puritans of New England founded towns and villages, drove out the Indians and felled the forests to make plough-lands and pasture, the French, much less numerous, were fur-traders and missionaries. They kept on good terms with the Indian trappers and tried to convert them to the Catholic faith.

English and French fishermen were constantly at loggerheads over the fishing rights of the Gulf of

St. Lawrence and of Newfoundland. Meanwhile, to compete with the French trappers in Canada, gentlemen of Charles II's Court, notably Prince Rupert, supported the English fur-traders of the *Hudson's Bay Company*.

DUTCH TRADERS IN THE EAST

During the reigns of James I and his son, Holland enjoyed a brief spell of wealth and power, for Spain had become weaker and France did not yet threaten.

For a time, the Dutch ruled the seas, taking most of the carrying-trade from English vessels and ousting the Portuguese from Ceylon and the Spice Islands. England had obtained a footing in the East Indies, but this was lost in 1623 when the Dutch massacred a number of English merchants at *Amboyna* to seize control of the spice trade.

The East India Company

Cromwell later obtained compensation for this long-remembered massacre, but the English *East India Company* had already turned its attention to the mainland of India. Trading stations, known as "factories", each with a fort to guard the warehouses, were set up at *Surat* and *Fort St. George*, Madras. Catherine of Braganza's dowry included the trading island of *Bombay*, and, from these small beginnings, the East India Company was one day to extend its rule across the length and breadth of India.

AN EAST INDIAMAN

CHAPTER 18

TWO PORTRAITS

(i)

A LOVE STORY

DURING the Civil War, Sir Peter Osborne held the island castle at Guernsey for the King, and his stout-hearted loyalty cost him his health and most of his fortune.

A Royalist family after the war

When the war was over, Sir Peter, lonely and forgotten, went back to his home at Chicksands Priory, in Bedfordshire. Part of his estate was restored to him through the influence of his wife's relatives on the Parliamentary side, but his wife was dead, and the ailing old cavalier was looked after by his youngest daughter, Dorothy. The Osbornes had been a large family, seven sons and five daughters, but only three sons were still living; the eldest was in Gloucestershire, Henry at Chicksands and the youngest, Robin, away from home. Dorothy's sisters

DOROTHY BEFORE COLONEL HAMMOND

were married and settled in distant parts of the country.

Dorothy Osborne was twenty-five when she came back to Chicksands. She was often lonely in the big house, with only servants to talk to, when her father kept to his room and her strict brother was away on business.

There were also long, empty days when Dorothy counted the hours until the carrier brought her the letters, and she ran upstairs to her room to break the seal of one more precious than all the rest. She was in love.

Some four years earlier, Dorothy and her brother were on their way to France, perhaps to visit their parents, since Sir Peter had retired to St. Malo after leaving Guernsey. While they waited for a ship at an inn on the Isle of Wight, Dorothy's brother amused himself by scratching, with a diamond, on a window-pane, a spiteful gibe at Colonel Hammond, Parliament's Governor of the island. It was dangerous at that time to show royalist sympathies, and the whole party, including several other travellers, was arrested.

When they were taken before the Governor, Dorothy pretended that she had committed the " crime ". The gallant colonel could not bring himself to punish a pretty young lady for such naughtiness, so all was forgiven and the party set at liberty.

William and Dorothy meet

Among the travellers was a young man named William Temple. Just down from Cambridge, he was about to set out on the continental tour that was part of a gentleman's education.

Dorothy's bold action so impressed this pleasant

young man that he fell head over heels in love with her, and she with him. Perhaps there were further delays on the journey, and time enough to enjoy walks and picnics. By the time they parted, William and Dorothy had promised to wait for each other until they could marry.

But these were difficult days for young lovers. Dorothy's father was a stubborn royalist and one of her brothers had died fighting for the King. The Osbornes were well-connected, but money for a dowry was not easy to come by, especially when the young man had no special distinction and no career as yet. Worse, his father, Sir John Temple, was a Parliamentarian who had sat in the Long Parliament; he held an important post in Ireland and already had plans for a good "match" for his son. Worst of all, William managed to arouse the dislike of Dorothy's brother Henry, who, as the son of a defeated cavalier, heartily loathed the other side and all their offspring. Dorothy's father was an invalid, so, as a dutiful daughter, she would accept her brother's authority. He loved her dearly but detested Temple.

Letters are exchanged

We do not know what happened during the first years of this strange courtship, but, in 1652, Dorothy was living at Chicksands and William Temple was in London, on the threshold of a diplomatic career. They wrote to each other every week, and, though William's letters were destroyed, Dorothy's were kept and have survived these three hundred years.

DOROTHY WRITES TO WILLIAM TEMPLE

WILLIAM TEMPLE

There was no official post in 1652, but letters went regularly by the carriers who trundled to and from London in their great waggons filled with goods and a few passengers. The Bedfordshire carriers set out for the capital on Monday mornings, and came back on Thursdays.

It was forty-two miles to London, and, since the waggon lumbered along hardly above walking pace, the journey took a full day. The carriers lodged at an inn in the City, where the letters were collected or were delivered by hand to William's lodging. Sometimes Dorothy addressed her letters to " Mrs. Painter, in Bedford Street, next the 'Goat' in Covent Garden ", sometimes to " Jones, the saddler, near Suffolk House " or to " Mr. Copyn of Fleet Street ".

The postal service

This postal service worked remarkably well. The reason was that the receiver paid for the letter when he collected it ; thus, inn-keepers and landladies would take good care of letters which were worth the fee and a tip as well. In two years, we hear of only one letter being lost, and we even find Dorothy complaining that eight days was too long for a letter to take between Dublin and Kent.

The Osbornes belonged to the upper class of society where marriages were arranged as business deals, without any consideration for love, which was expected to come after marriage, but rarely before. The girl was given a dowry or "portion", which would become her husband's property, but the young man must provide her with a "jointure", that is, property that would bring in an income if he died.

In the letters, we constantly hear of rich old men looking for young brides and of penniless gallants trying to win wealthy widows. Dorothy

A CARRIER AND HIS WAGGON

knew all about the marriage industry, for she had many admirers, whom she called " servants ", and she was forever teasing William about the chances she was missing for his sake.

The most notable of her suitors was Henry Cromwell, second son of the great General. His father was not yet Lord Protector, but he was already the greatest man in the land, and Henry had ability and charm. Dorothy would not have him, and he soon married another, but when she heard how Cromwell had turned out the Long Parliament, she could not help reminding Temple of what her position would have been if she " had been so wise as to have taken hold of the offer made me by Henry Cromwell ".

England was not quite as gloomy under the Protector as some have imagined. Certainly the theatres were closed, the Sabbath was strictly observed and many sports were frowned upon, but people managed to enjoy themselves.

Dorothy herself acted in a play and sometimes went riding in Hyde Park. She put on a mask and went to the Spring Gardens, where the gallants showed off their clothes and sat with their ladies at pavilions among the trees and bushes. A lady whom she knew was mad about horse-racing, which Cromwell himself liked, though not as much as hunting.

STUART FURNITURE : A BED AND FOOTSTOOL

Dorothy tells Temple not to get overheated at tennis, a game objected to by some of the stricter Puritans who, in 1654, petitioned :

> " to prohibit Charles Gibbins, a tennis-court keeper from erecting another tennis-court to the disturbance of his neighbours and ill example of others in this time of reformation ".

James I had brought golf from Scotland, and this was very much an aristocratic game which Charles I and his sons played during the war. We find Dorothy playing Battledore and Shuttlecock, a fore-

JOHN MILTON

runner of badminton, and all the rage in fashionable circles.

Even the Cromwells were known to enjoy themselves, since they had gone up in the world. Oliver was an affectionate father, milder to his daughters than to his sons, who, he suspected, were not as deeply religious as he would have wished. Bridget, the eldest girl, who married General Ireton, was as solemn a Puritan wife as Mistress Cromwell herself, but the others were lively to a degree that scandalised the Puritan matrons. Elizabeth Claypole, Oliver's favourite, was the most daring, with her curls and naughty wit, her silk petticoats and bold laughter. The two youngest daughters married into the aristocracy, Mary to Lord Fauconberg, a royalist nobleman, and Frances to Lord Warwick's grandson. The festivities at their double-wedding caused some eye-raising on account of the finery and the dancing all-night to the music of 48 violins.

In truth, England was forgetting the bitterness of the war as fast as she could. The Protector's son had courted a royalist's daughter, and Dorothy's brother-in-law, Sir Thomas Peyton, who had headed a royalist rising in Kent, was now safe and prosperous. We find him living in great style, and Dorothy complaining that she had never visited such a noisy, crowded household in her life.

PASSENGER BOATS ON THE THAMES

Travel in the seventeenth century

When she went down to Kent, she made the better part of the journey by water, on the Thames to Gravesend. This was the popular and speedy way to travel, though not all roads were as bad as the route to Ireland. William's journey from London took four days to Chester, and on the road across Wales, passengers walked while their coach was taken to pieces and carried on the shoulders of peasants from Conway to the Menai Straits.

Regular stage-coach services were not yet operating, but Dorothy was able to use the hackney-coaches in London. For longer journeys, people rode on horseback or in private coaches. Henry Osborne noted in his diary :

> " We came to Chicksands (from London) in a coach of Jack Peters, at thirty-five shillings, and six horses."

The romance between Dorothy and William Temple survived all these comings and goings, all the difficulties and rival suitors, even her brother's opposition. Dorothy's letters were full of gossip and little jokes ; she mentioned the books she read, long romantic French novels in many volumes which were all the fashion, and sometimes a travel book about China, but she only mentions Shakespeare once and has never a word for John Milton, the great Puritan poet. Temple sent her some seals which ladies were wearing for ornaments, and some orange-water, doubtless used as scent, but she took little interest in clothes, far less than Mr. Pepys, ten years later.

At last, the skies cleared. Sir Peter Osborne died, and Dorothy left Chicksands for ever. Her brother, who had called Temple "the proudest, imperious, insulting, ill-natured man that ever was", must

A HACKNEY-COACH

have withdrawn his opposition, for the marriage " treaty " was at last arranged.

Dorothy had her ring and went to London with Lady Peyton to buy her trousseau. They stayed at a house in Drury Lane, but small-pox being there, they moved to another lodging. Soon Dorothy herself was unwell, and on 9th November, William learned that she had the dreaded small-pox.

A happy ending

Dorothy recovered, but her beauty was gone, and we do not know if she ever regained it. But faithful William had waited for seven years, and he loved her for deeper reasons than the beauty of her face. They were married on Christmas Day 1654, and Dorothy, who was to be wife of a successful diplomat and mother of seven children, wrote no more letters for us to read.

(ii)

THE PRUDENT CAVALIER

JOHN EVELYN

Mr. John Evelyn was a Royalist cavalier, of a very different type from Sir Peter Osborne. He was twenty-two when the Civil War broke out, but, although unmarried and well-to-do, he did not hurry to the King's side. Only after Edgehill, when the Royalist army had approached London, did he manage to arrive with horse and arms, in time for the retreat from Brentford and Turnham Green.

The King's headquarters were at Oxford, his strength in the West and North, but Mr. Evelyn's estate was in Surrey, so he decided that fighting for the King " would have left both me and my brothers exposed to ruin, without any advantage to his Majesty ".

This was both true and sensible. The prudent cavalier obtained permission to leave the kingdom to travel abroad. While the royal infantry struggled and died at Marston Moor and Naseby, while the sons of gentlemen charged with Rupert and Goring, Evelyn was making a leisurely tour of Europe, in the style suitable for a man of means.

It was a pleasant trip that lasted for four years. He visited Flanders, Holland, France, and Italy. Sometimes, he and his companions slept " in damask beds and were treated like Emperors ", sometimes " we footed it thro' pleasant fields and meadows, sometimes we played at cards, while others sung or were composing verses ".

Evelyn's travels abroad

But Evelyn had a mind above mere pleasure. He called on men of learning and distinction, he visited churches, fortifications and ruins. He saw the Pope in Rome, peered down the crater of Vesuvius, admired the gardens, grottoes and quaint fountains of noble estates, and even tried his hand at wine-making. In France, he saw Louis XIV, " like a young Apollo, in a suit so covered with embroidery that one could perceive nothing of the stuff under it ".

There was no time to spare a thought for the fate of Englishmen at home.

The end of the First Civil War found Evelyn in Paris, where he married Mary, daughter of Sir Richard Browne, ambassador to the exiled Stuart Court. Mary was only twelve years old and Evelyn nearly twenty-seven, so, as was customary, he left her with her mother, and crossed to England to see to his affairs and to prepare a home.

In London, the Roundheads were in power, but the returned Cavalier found his estate in good order and went quietly about his business. When Charles I was beheaded, Evelyn stayed indoors and " would not be present at that execrable wickedness ".

EVELYN VISITED ITALY AND SAW THE CRATER OF VESUVIUS

Evelyn thoroughly disliked the victorious " rebels ", the Puritans, the Quakers, " a new fanatic sect of dangerous principles ", and the " ignorant tradesmen and mechanics " who preached from the pulpits. He was true to the Church of England, though its services were forbidden, and he had to have his first-born christened at home in the library. He was horrified that " there was no more notice taken of Christmas Day in the churches ", but on Christmas Day 1657, he and some " persons of quality " attended a service in church and were about to take Holy Communion when they found the place surrounded by soldiers, who entered the church " as if they would have shot us at the altar ". The congregation was arrested, some were taken to prison, but after much hostile questioning, Evelyn got off with a warning.

Puritan rule

Young Mrs. Evelyn was now in England, at their new home at Sayes Court in Deptford, which was then a pleasant country place. The manor-house had a hall, parlour, kitchen, buttery, dairy and cellars, and its garden was to become one of the sights of England, with its hedges, lawns, terraces, rare trees and flowers, its orchards and herb garden, all planned and laid out by Evelyn himself.

From Sayes Court, in a coach and four, the married

SAYES COURT, EVELYN'S HOME

couple set out on a tour of England. They went to Windsor, where King Charles' body lay, to Bath, where John bathed in the well-known " cross-bath ", to Oxford, Salisbury, Stonehenge, Worcester, across the Midlands into Yorkshire, and home via Cambridge, passing close to Chicksands where Dorothy Osborne was, at that moment, probably writing to William Temple. Like Dorothy, Evelyn hardly mentions a sign of the late war, only that Lord Craven's home was in ruins, and that they found an uncle of his wife's living in his Gatehouse because he had burnt down his mansion, rather than let the " rebels " turn it into a garrison.

After Cromwell died, Evelyn grew bolder, like many others who saw that the Protector's power had died with him. He wrote " An Apology for the Royal Party " and a printed answer to an attack on Charles II. More daring, he tried to persuade Colonel Morley, Lieutenant of the Tower, to declare for the King, " to the great hazard of my life, but the Colonel had been my school-fellow, and I knew would not betray me."

Restoration of Charles II

Thus, when Charles II entered London in triumph, Evelyn " stood in the Strand and beheld it, and blessed God ". Well he might, for within a week, he was at Court, " being very graciously received ", and was soon given a number of appointments suitable for a man of taste and education. He was now 40, and had come through England's troubles wisely and well, at the cost to himself of the horse that he sent to Charles I before going abroad.

Evelyn's Diary is important not so much for what it describes, for Pepys's is much more entertaining, but for the picture it gives us of the mind and interests of a seventeenth-century gentleman.

Though a royalist and a staunch Church of England man, John Evelyn was by temperament a Puritan.

STUART FURNITURE

The Court of Charles II

Cautious, methodical and sober, he was far removed from the dare-devil, hard-drinking cavaliers of Goring's Horse. Drunkenness he regarded as "a barbarous custom", and the behaviour of the Court and the tone of the newly-opened theatre filled him with disgust. Gambling seemed to him "a horrid vice, and unsuitable in a Christian Court", and the sight of Mistress Nelly Gwynne, "an impudent comedian", looking over her garden wall and holding a saucy conversation with the King, made him "heartily sorry". It pained him and he could "never forget the inexpressible luxury and profaneness, gaming and all dissoluteness, and total forgetfulness of God" which he saw at Court, where Charles reclined among his gorgeous ladies, listening to a French boy singing love-songs, while a group of courtiers gambled at a table with £2,000 in front of them.

NELL GWYNNE

Yet Evelyn could never bring himself to quit the Court he so despised. Royal favour conferred the appointments that kept him at the centre of affairs. He never craved for money or titles; he had no ambition except to be busy and well-informed. All his work was for the good of his fellow-men, for he was a Commissioner for reforming the streets and buildings of London, for regulating farming, forestry, the Mint and various charities, and for caring for the sick and wounded in the Dutch Wars. He knew everyone of importance, conferred with Christopher Wren about St. Paul's, discussed science with Prince Rupert and Robert Boyle, and brought to the world's notice a young man named Grinling Gibbon whom he discovered carving a crucifix in "a poor solitary thatched house in a field in our parish, near Sayes Court".

A PANEL CARVED BY GRINLING GIBBON

CHRISTOPHER WREN

Evelyn's greatest interest was the Royal Society. He was one of the founder-members of this famous society "for Improving Natural Knowledge", which Charles II sponsored and which still flourishes today.

The discoveries of foreign astronomers, notably Copernicus and Kepler, in the previous century, and of Galileo, the great Italian scientist, who died in 1642, had opened a new world of knowledge. Sir Francis Bacon, of James I's reign, had taught men to think scientifically, and the new King and his cousin Rupert were interested in science. Charles had a laboratory in Whitehall, here Pepys saw "a great many chymical glasses and things", and the King also possessed one of the new telescopes through which he watched an eclipse. Robert Boyle and Isaac Newton, the great scientists, and Christopher Wren, the man of all talents, were some of the earliest members of the Royal Society to which Evelyn and Pepys were so proud to belong.

The interests of a seventeenth-century gentleman

At the meetings of the Society, the leading men of the day interested themselves in every addition to knowledge—ships, rigging, coaches, tree-planting, engraving, medicine, stars, clocks, sea-water, and natural history. They examined, discussed and held experiments—"I waited on Prince Rupert to our Assembly, where we tried several experiments in Mr. Boyle's 'vacuum'. A man thrusting in his arm, upon exhaustion of the air, had his flesh immediately swelled so as the blood was near bursting the veins; he drawing it out, we found it all speckled."

The workings of the human body, in particular were only beginning to be understood, for the Church had long frowned upon enquiry into God's creation. William Harvey attended the great medical school at Padua, in Italy, to study anatomy, and he was

NEWTON'S TELESCOPE

WILLIAM HARVEY

later to be Charles I's physician and the discoverer of how blood circulates in men's bodies.

The friend of Sir Christopher Wren had almost as many talents as the great architect, who was also astronomer, mathematician, inventor. Evelyn wrote plays, poems and books on such varied subjects as smoke abatement in London, trees, copper-engraving, cider, women's fashions, medals, architecture and children's education. He was the chief authority on trees and gardens in England, and his home at Sayes Court was a show-place without equal. When Peter the Great came to England to study shipbuilding, he was lent Sayes Court as a residence, but, to Evelyn's sorrow, the wild Russians did much damage. Even the famous holly-hedge did not escape, for the Csar took delight in charging through it in a wheel-barrow.

Science and superstition

But there is something about the virtuous, sober Evelyn that checks our sympathy and marks him off from our own times. He seems just a little too self-satisfied for us to love him. And in the refined man of science, there lurked enough of the old medieval superstition for him to wonder if storms, floods, comets in the sky, the Thames frozen over or a whale washed ashore were not sinister omens. Much of his curiosity shows a simplicity of mind that we would laugh at today—the tight-rope walker, the hairy woman, the thinking dog and the water-swallower interest him as much as a diving-bell or Mr. Palmer's clocks and pendules.

The seventeenth-century gentleman, who loved science and music, went to the Bear Garden to see cock-fighting, dog-fighting, bull- and bear-baiting. He protested that these were " butcherly sports ", but he went. Several times he attended public executions, and once saw a man hanged in his cloak and hat, who was first stunned and then had his throat cut.

The working of the guillotine and the sawing-off of a sailor's leg interested Evelyn. In Paris, he could bring himself to watch a thief being tortured until his limbs stretched and his joints cracked.

Kindness towards children, love and gentleness between husband and wife, were more common than in Tudor days. Life was more comfortable, homes were warmer and better furnished, people behaved less savagely towards each other in their daily lives, but, under the surface, lurked this violence and cruelty.

We may leave Evelyn as an old man of more than 80, walking in his beautiful garden, musing on his books, the weather, science and the mercy of God. But we must not forget that beneath his world of elegance and learning, beneath the solid prosperity of business-house and country manor, was a huge class of poor people, living like desperate brutes in the hovels and alleys of the capital, who hardly enter the pages of his Diary.

SUMMARY

Dates	Kings & Queens	Events	People
1485	Henry VII	Battle of Bosworth	
1486		Cape of Good Hope reached	Diaz
1491		War with France	Charles VIII
1492		Discovery of New World	Columbus
1497		Newfoundland discovered	John Cabot
1497–8		Voyage to India	da Gama
1498		Perkin Warbeck executed	
1509	Henry VIII		Wolsey
1513		Battle of Flodden	
1519		Magellan's Voyage	Luther
		Conquest of Mexico	Cortes
1520		Field of the Cloth of Gold	Francis I
			Emperor Charles V
1527		The Divorce Question	Sir Thomas More
1534		Act of Supremacy	Calvin
1536–40		Dissolution of the Monasteries	Thomas Cranmer
1536		Pilgrimage of Grace	Thomas Cromwell
1542		Battle of Solway Moss	
1543		Debasement of the Coinage	
1544		War with France	
1547	Edward VI		Protector Somerset
1549		Edward VI's First Prayer Book	Ridley
1549		Kett's Rising	
1552		The Second Prayer Book	Northumberland
		Willoughby's Expedition	Chancellor
			Sebastian Cabot
1553	Mary	Lady Jane Grey proclaimed	
1554		Wyatt's Rebellion	Philip II of Spain
1556		Cranmer executed	Cardinal Pole
1558		Calais lost	
1558	Elizabeth I		William Cecil
1561		Mary Stuart in Scotland	John Knox
1567		Murder of Darnley	
1568		Mary escapes to England	William the Silent
1569		Rising of the Northern Earls	John Hawkins
1570		Elizabeth excommunicated	Walsingham
1572		Massacre of St. Bartholomew's Eve	
1577–80		Drake sails round World	

Dates	Kings & Queens	Events	People
1583		Gilbert's voyage to Newfoundland	
1585		Attempt to colonise Virginia	Raleigh
		English force in Netherlands	Leicester
1587		Execution of Mary, Queen of Scots	
1587		Attack on Cadiz	
1588		Armada defeated	Lord Howard
1595		Raleigh in Guiana	
1596		Cadiz captured	
1599		Rising in Ireland	Tyrone-Essex
1600		East India Company	
1601		The Great Poor Law	Shakespeare
1603	James VI & I		Robert Cecil
1604		Hampton Court Conference	
		Peace with Spain	
1605		Gunpowder Plot	Catesby, Fawkes
1607		Virginia colonised	John Smith
1617		Raleigh executed	Francis Bacon
1618		Outbreak of Thirty Years' War	
1620		"*Mayflower*" sails to New England	
1623		Failure of "Spanish Match"	Buckingham
1625	Charles I	War with Spain	Richelieu
1627		War with France	Sir John Eliot
1628		Petition of Right	
1629–40		Rule without Parliament	Archbishop Laud
1637		Trial of John Hampden	Wentworth (Strafford)
1639		War with the Scots	Alexander Leslie
1640		The Short Parliament	John Pym
		Second Bishops' War	
1641		Execution of Strafford	
1642		Battle of Edgehill; Turnham Green	Earl of Essex
1643		Bristol captured	Prince Rupert
		Siege of Gloucester	
1644		Newark; Marston Moor	Fairfax
		Lostwithiel; Newbury	Cromwell
1645		The New Model Army	Montrose
		Naseby	

Dates	Kings & Queens	Events	People
1646		Charles surrenders to Scots	
1648		Second Civil War	Colonel Pride
1649	The Commonwealth	Execution of Charles I	
		Drogheda captured	Ormonde
1650		Dunbar	David Leslie
1651		Battle of Worcester	
1652–54		Dutch War	Blake, Van Tromp
1653	The Protectorate	"Instrument of Government"	
1654		The Major-Generals	
		War with Spain	Cardinal Mazarin
1658		Death of Cromwell	Richard Cromwell
1660	Charles II	Clarendon Code	General Monk
1665–67		First Dutch War	Bunyan Samuel Pepys
1666		Fire of London	Christopher Wren
1668		Triple Alliance	Louis XIV
1670		Treaty of Dover	
1672–74		Second Dutch War	William of Orange
1673		Test Act	Shaftesbury
1678		The Popish Plot	Titus Oates
1681		The Oxford Parliament	
1683		Rye House Plot	
1685	James II	Monmouth's Rebellion	Argyll
1688		Trial of the Seven Bishops "The Glorious Revolution"	Judge Jeffreys
1689	William & Mary		

INDEX

A

Act of Supremacy, 22
Adwalton Moor, 143
Alva, Duke of, 54, 64
Amboyna, 186
Anne Boleyn, 20, 22, 28, 50
Anne of Cleves, 29, 30
Argyll, 177
Armada, 64–68
Arminians, 119, 128
Aske, Robert, 25

B

Babington, Anthony, 62
Bacon, Francis, 79, 199
Barebone's Parliament, 160
Basing House, 139, 149
Bath, 197
Bible, 28, 31, 36
Bishops' Wars, 124–126
Blake, Robert, 161, 162, 164
Boston, 183
Breda, Treaty of, 169, 184
Brentford, 138, 194
Bristol, 47, 74, 100, 134, 149
Buckingham, Duke of, 113, 115, 116, 118
Bunyan, John, 169
Burghley, *see* Cecil, William

C

Cabot, John, 47, 59
Cabot, Sebastian, 48, 59
Calais, 37, 50
Calvin, John, 19, 52
Carolina, 182, 183
Cartier, Jacques, 46
Catherine Howard, 30
Catherine of Aragon, 11–13, 16, 19–22, 28, 33,
Catherine of Braganza, 174, 186
Cavendish, Thomas, 70
Cecil, Robert, 108
Cecil, William, 52, 55, 62, 66, 72
Chalgrove Field, 143
Chancellor, Richard, 49, 59
Charles I, 113–155, 160, 195
Charles II, 149, 156, 158, 166–176, 197–199
Charles V, 15, 16, 21, 43
Chatham, 169, 170
Churchill, John, 181
Clarendon Code, 168, 184
clothes, 87–89
coaches, 193, 199
Columbus, Christopher, 41–42
Commonwealth, 156–176
Connecticut, 183
Cortes, Hernando, 44
Covenant, 124, 125, 152, 158, 173
Coverdale, Miles, 28, 33
Cranmer, Thomas, 22, 28, 32–33, 35, 36–38
crime, 77
Cromwell, Oliver, 133, 136, 138, 139, 143–149, 151, 153, 155–165, 168, 186, 191, 192, 197
Cromwell, Richard, 164–165
Cromwell, Thomas, 23–24, 28, 29

D

Darnley, Lord, 53, 106
Davis, John, 60, 70
Declaration of Indulgence, 173, 180
de Witt, 173
Diaz, Bartholomew, 40
Digby, George, 129, 147, 149
Dover, Treaty of, 173
Drake, Sir Francis, 58–59, 64, 66, 68–70, 72
Drogheda, 157
Dunbar, 158
Dunkirk, 64, 164
Dutch, *see* Holland

E

East India Company, 70
Edgehill, 135–136, 142, 194
Edward VI, 29, 32–34, 38, 49
Eliot, Sir John, 116, 119, 121
Elizabeth I, 28, 34, 37–72, 75, 86, 88, 104, 111, 182
Enclosures, 73, 74

Essex, Earl of (Robert Devereux), 69, 71
Essex, Earl of (son of above), 133, 135, 136, 138, 143, 146, 147, 168
Evelyn, John, 194–201

F

Fairfax, Thomas, 131, 139, 143, 147–149, 151, 154, 158
farming, 73, 78
Fawkes, Guy, 108–109
Field of the Cloth of Gold, 15
Fire of London, 171–172
Fisher, John, 23
Flanders, 9, 11, 15, 19, 164, 195
Flodden, 14
food, 89–91
France, 10, 11, 12, 13, 15, 29–31, 33, 45, 46, 50, 52, 53, 55, 116, 117, 172–173, 176, 195
friars, 17
Frobisher, Martin, 49, 57, 59–60, 66, 68, 69

G

Gama, Vasco da, 42–43
games, 96–97, 191
gardens, 82–83, 200
Genoa, 11, 40, 41, 46
Germany, 11, 19, 21, 29, 112, 115, 118
Gibbon, Grinling, 198
Gilbert, Sir Humphrey, 59–60, 69, 79
Gloucester, 144, 145
Gondomar, 113
Goring, Lord George, 146, 148, 149, 195, 198
Grand Remonstrance, 128
Grenville, Sir Richard, 60, 68, 69
Grey, Lady Jane, 33–34
Gwynne, Nell, 198

H

Hampden, John, 121, 126, 128, 129, 133, 136, 143, 168
Hampton Court Conference, 107
Hanse, 11, 47
Harvey, William, 199, 200
Hawkins, John, 57, 58, 61, 66, 68, 69
Hawkins, William, 48, 57
Heads of the Proposals, 152
Henrietta Maria, 114, 116, 127, 130, 131, 142, 144, 145, 184
Henry VII, 9–11, 39, 41, 46–47
Henry VIII, 12–32, 38, 47–49, 50
Holland (*see also* Netherlands), 131, 161, 166, 169, 172, 173, 183, 184, 186, 195
homes, 80–86, 196
Hooper, John, 33, 36
Hopton, Sir Ralph, 142, 149
hospitals, 77
Hudson, Henry, 60
Hudson's Bay Company, 186
Huguenots, 53, 56, 58, 95, 172
Hull, 131, 132, 143–145

I

India, 39, 40, 42–43, 70, 186
indulgences, 18
industry, 95–96
Instrument of Government, 161, 162
Ireland, 9, 67, 70–72, 123, 128, 147, 156–158
Ireton, General, 148, 157, 168, 192
Italy, 11, 12, 16, 19, 195

J

Jamaica, 164
James IV, 11, 14
James V, 30
James VI and I, 53, 72, 106–113
James II of England, 169, 174, 176–181, 184, 185
Jane Seymour, 29
Jeffreys, Judge, 178

K

Kett, Robert, 32
Knox, John, 52, 124

L

Langport, 149
La Salle, René, 185

Latimer, Hugh, 35, 36
Laud, William, 119, 122, 123, 127, 128, 130, 151, 183
Leicester, Earl of, 55, 56, 64, 72
Leslie, David, 158
Limerick, 157
livery and maintenance, 10
London, 11, 34, 36, 73, 74, 100, 105, 123, 125–127, 129–132, 142, 147, 150, 151, 170, 174, 190, 194, 198
Lostwithiel, 146
Louis XIV, 172, 175, 181, 195
Louisiana, 185
Luther, 18–19, 21, 31

M

Madras, 186
Magellan, Ferdinand, 43–44
Manchester, Earl of, 133, 143, 146, 147
Margaret Tudor, 11
marriage, 75, 190–191
Marston Moor, 141, 145, 195
Maryland, 184
Mary of England, 33–37
Mary of Orange, 180
Mary, Queen of Scots, 30, 50–53, 56, 62–63, 106
Massachusetts, 183
"*Mayflower*", 183
Mazarin, Cardinal, 164, 172
Mexico, 44
Milton, John, 193
monasteries, 17, 23–26, 28
Monk, General, 166
Monmouth, Duke of, 175, 177–178
monopolies, 72, 111, 120
Montrose, Marquis of, 147, 149, 158
More, Sir Thomas, 22–23
music, 98, 100

N

Naseby, 148, 195
Navigation Acts, 161
Netherlands (*see also* Holland), 54, 64, 161, 172
Newark, 145, 149
Newbury, 140, 145, 146
Newcastle, Earl of, 142–146, 148
New England, 184, 185
Newfoundland, 47, 186
New Model Army, 141, 147, 148, 150, 151, 153, 157, 166
Newton, Isaac, 199
New York, 184
Norfolk, Dukes of, 20, 62
Northumberland, Duke of, 33–34, 49

O

Oates, Titus, 174, 175
O'Neal, Hugh, 71
Ormonde, Earl of, 147, 156
Osborne, Dorothy, 187–194
Oxford, 138, 140, 144–146, 148, 149, 174, 179, 194

P

Parliament, 22, 24, 35–38, 63, 72, 110–113, 115, 116, 118–121, 123, 124, 126–133, 139, 142, 145–153, 159–163, 165–168, 174, 175, 177, 179
Parma, Duke of, 64–66
Penn, Admiral, 164
Pennsylvania, 184, 185
Pepys, Samuel, 170, 197, 199
Peru, 45
Petition of Right, 118
Philip II, 35–37, 50–51, 54, 55, 63, 65, 67, 68, 72
Philiphaugh, 149
Pilgrimage of Grace, 24
Pilgrim Fathers, 183
Pizarro, Francisco, 45
plague, 103, 170–171
Plymouth, 57, 65, 74, 144, 183
Pole, Cardinal, 36
Poor Law, 77
Pope, the, 17, 20–22, 27, 30, 31, 35, 38, 42, 62, 195
Portsmouth, 47, 56, 118
Portugal, 40–44, 46, 49, 56, 64, 68, 163, 174, 186
postal service, 190
Powicke Bridge, 135

Prayer book, 32, 33, 38, 124
Preston, 153
Pride's Purge, 153
Pym, John, 125, 126, 128, 129, 132, 139, 140, 142, 144, 146

Q

Quakers, 184, 185, 196
Quebec, 185

R

Raleigh, Sir Walter, 60, 69, 70, 79, 182
Rebellion of the Northern Earls, 62, 75
Reformation, 19, 27, 28, 31–33, 37–38
Rhode Island, 183
Richelieu, Cardinal, 116, 172
Ridley, Nicholas, 33, 35, 36
Ridolfi, 62
Rogers, John, 28, 36
Root and Branch Bill, 128
Roundway Down, 144
Royal Society, 199
Rump Parliament, 153, 156, 159, 161, 165
Rupert, 131, 134–136, 138, 141, 142, 143, 145–149, 186, 195, 198, 199
Rut, John, 48
Rye House Plot, 175

S

sanitation, 85–86
Santa Cruz, 164
schools, 92–94
Scotland, 11, 19, 30, 52, 53, 123–126, 128, 129, 144, 145, 147, 149, 153, 158
Sea Beggars, 54, 56
Shaftesbury, Earl of, 173–175
Ship Money, 120
ships, 13, 31, 41, 47, 48, 49, 57, 199
Skippon, Philip, 132, 138, 148
Solway Moss, 30
Somerset, Duke of, 32–33
Spain, 15, 19, 29, 35, 37, 41–46, 49, 54–58, 64–69, 112, 113, 116, 118, 163
Star Chamber, 10, 121, 127
Strafford, Earl of, 123–127, 135
Sweden, 124, 163, 172

T

Temple, William, 188–194
Test Act, 173, 179
theatres, 103–105
Thirty Years' War, 112
Tories, 173, 175–177, 179, 180
trade, 11, 39, 48, 49, 56, 74, 95
Triple Alliance, 172
tunnage and poundage, 116, 119, 120
Tyndale, William, 28
Tyrone, Earl of, 71

U

unemployment, 76–77

V

Venice, 11, 40, 43, 46
Verney, Sir Edmund, 136, 141, 142
Virginia, 69, 182, 183

W

Wales, 73, 135, 142, 147, 193
Walsingham, Sir Francis, 53, 54, 62, 64, 66, 72
Warbeck, Perkin, 11
Warwick, Earl of, 134, 147
Wentworth, Thomas, *see* Strafford
Wexford, 157
Whigs, 173–175, 177
William of Orange (Wm. III), 173, 180, 181
William the Silent, 54, 64
Willoughby, Sir Hugh, 49, 59
Winceby, 144
Wolsey, Thomas, 14–17, 20, 21, 23, 48
Worcester, 135, 159
Wren, Sir Christopher, 171, 198, 199, 200
Wyatt, Sir Thomas, 36–37

Y

York, 9, 25, 74, 131, 133, 134, 142, 145